UNSEALING

THE BOOK

An Overview of the Book of Revelation

EDWARD S ASATO

A Resource of Exodus Book Publication

UNSEALING THE BOOK
An Exodus Book Publication

First Printing: February 2013
Second Printing: August 2013

Published by Exodus Book Publishing
635 South Hina Avenue
Kahului, HI 96732

Printed in the United States of America

ISBN 978-0-6157-6990-5

Introduction

Have you ever asked yourself, "Why are there so many global crises?"

Worldwide terrorism! Nuclear Iran! Euro-debt crisis! Drug and sex-trade trafficking! Mid-East War and World War III threat! Shocking tsunamis and earthquakes! Pandemics! Global awakening of Christianity! Unprecedented assault on Christian values!

Can sense be made of these events? Is there a source to teach us what is going on?

Is there a Biblical Joseph who can interpret these events to understand what is happening, foretell the future and tell us how to prepare?

Did you know that God declared today's media headlines over 2,000 years ago to John, Jesus' beloved apostle, in the Book of Revelation?

Here are some examples and where they are found:

Revival in the Christian church? Revelation 11,14.
Bizarre weather patterns? Revelation 6.
Assault on the Christian church? Revelation 6,11-13.
Attacks on traditional values? Revelation 17,18.
Nuclear crisis & World War III? Revelation 9,19.
Worldwide famine and pandemics? Revelation 6.
Global economic crisis? Read Revelation 6.
Economic union of nations? Revelation 13,17,18.
The 2nd Coming & world peace? Revelation 19,20.
The New Jerusalem on earth? Revelation 21,22.

This writing contends that Revelation lays out the future in a systematic, and chronological fashion. The Table of Content gives a quick overview for the uninitiated, the Summary allows for swift reading for the curious, and the chapters provide insightful instruction for the student. For the serious student, the Appendix is designed to stimulate your interest in prophetic themes.

This material is written to provide something for everyone, and especially to assist everyone in understanding the unprecedented times in which we live.

"I Wonder If....

"... earth's future is predicted in this book?"

"... today's global crisis are described in Revelation?"

"... God wants me to know what the future holds?"

"... I'll know what happens to the Church?

"... cataclysmic events will increase and worsen?"

"... God sovereignly controls global events?"

"... I'll know when Jesus Christ will return to earth?"

"... I can understand the Book of Revelation?"

"... there's a purpose for prophecy being revealed?"

"... churches should be interested in this Book?"

"... worldwide revival is predicted in Revelation?"

"... this world's corrupt systems will be destoyed?"

"...there is an Armageddon?"

"... there is a 2nd Coming of Jesus Christ?"

"... the world will be different after Jesus returns?"

"... I can know what heaven will be like?"

If you've ever wondered about these questions, they are answered in reading this book explaining the Book of Revelation.

Summary of Chapters

"I Wonder If...I Can Understand the Book of Revelation?"
Chapter 1 - Understanding Revelation (Introduction)
Revelation is simple and chronological. It interweaves Old Testament images so the simple and serious can understand.

"I Wonder If...There's a Purpose for Revealed Prophecy?"
Chapter 2 - Jesus and His Church (Revelation 1)
Jesus is a compassionate but fearsome judge. He is working to fulfill His *Church's* destiny. Both are the focus of this book.

"I Wonder If... Churches Should be Interested in this Book?"
Chapter 3 - The Seven Churches (Revelation 2 & 3)
Seven types of churches are described existing in the first century, in the seven periods of church history and as seven different types of churches currently operating in our world.

"I Wonder If... God Sovereignly Controls Global Events?"
Chapter 4 - Heaven & Jesus Christ (Revelation 4 & 5)
We peek into heaven's worship and see Jesus, the Lamb, who controls and unveils three sets of seven last day judgments.

"I Wonder If...Today's Crisis are Described in this Book?"
Chapter 5 - The 7-Sealed Judgments (Revelation 6)
The Seal Judgments open with the white horse of the Protestant Reformation, the 3rd seal of monetary inflation, the 5th seal of persecution and martyrdom of believers and the 6th seal of devastating phenomenon of nature.

"I Wonder If...I can Know What will Happen to Believers?"
Chapter 6 - Protection of the Believers (Revelation 7)
This chapter describes the other side of the 5th seal's persecution of believers and reveals God's protection of believers amidst His judgments against the world.

"I Wonder If...Earth's history is predicted in this Book?"

Chapter 7 - 7-Trumpet Judgments (Revelation 8-10)

These Trumpet Judgments release plagues similar to those unleashed on Egypt in the exodus of Israel. Jesus leads His church as Moses led Israel into their promised future destiny.

"I Wonder If...I'll Recognize the Major Last Day Events?"

Chapter 8 - 3.5 Years of Tribulation (Revelation 11-13)

The first 3.5 years of Daniel's last week was fulfilled in Jesus' ministry. The second 3.5 years period is marked by the three major events described in Revelation 11, 12 & 13.

"I Wonder If...The Worldwide Harvest has been Predicted?"

Chapter 9 - Two Global Harvests (Revelation 14)

Two worldwide harvests are described: 1) A mighty harvest of souls swept into God's kingdom and 2) A great harvest of ungodly souls set for judgment.

"I Wonder If...Cataclysmic Events will Increase & Worsen?"

Chapter 10 - The 7-Vial Judgments (Revelation 15,16)

The final Seven Vial Judgments, akin to the plagues on Egypt, but far more devastating and destructive, is the prelude to the 2nd coming of Jesus.

"I Wonder If...The World's Systems will be Destroyed?"

Chapter 11 – Global Judgment (Revelation 17 & 18)

The Seven Vial Judgments describe the crushing of an unparalleled morally perverse world and its accompanying global corrupt monetary system.

"I Wonder If...There will be an Armageddon?"

"I Wonder If...There will be a 2nd Coming of Christ?"

Chapter 12-Armageddon & 2nd Coming (Revelation 19)

The final battle against and defeat of the anti-Christ system in the war of Armageddon and the 2nd Coming of Christ to the world is described.

"I Wonder If…The World really will be Different?"

Chapter 13 - Millennium & Judgment (Revelation 20)

The 1,000-year reign of Jesus Christ on planet earth, life as God intended it to be lived and the great white throne judgment of unbelievers is recorded here.

"I Wonder If…I can know what heaven will be like?"

Chapter 14-New Heaven & Earth (Revelation 21 & 22)

The creation of the new heaven and new earth, the descent of the New Jerusalem to earth and the establishing of God's kingdom is seen. God completes His original intent for mankind as recorded in Genesis 1&2.

Table of Contents

Appendices

CHAPTER ONE

"I Wonder If I Can Understand The Book of Revelation?"

UNDERSTANDING REVELATION

Summary: The Book of Revelation is prophetic in nature, simple to understand and chronological in sequence.

Revelation contains more than a blessing. It is a prophetic peek into future events that will fill the headlines of tomorrow's news.

Revelation was intended to be simple to understand and Biblically and intellectually consistent.

Our Approach

As we study this book, you will notice that its content is primarily prophetic. It contains some history, but it deals mainly with future events. (1:19)

Until the time of John's exile, future events were sealed or hidden. The Lord said to Daniel, "Seal the book, even to the time of the end!" (Daniel 12:4) God purposely hid the revelation of prophetic events from the understanding of his prophets preventing them to understand them.

Then, in the book of Revelation, God declared to John that the books were unsealed. "Do not seal the words of the prophecy of this book, for the time is at hand!" (Revelation 22:10) The day had come for the unveiling of future events. John had the privilege of being the messenger to convey those insights.

But only One had the privilege of actually "unsealing the book". That One was Jesus Christ. He is presented as the Lamb-Lion - a sacrificial Lamb who gave His life and a Lion who rules as the King and Judge of the world.

As a Lamb who gave His life, He is the only one "worthy" to open the Seven-Sealed Book. (5:1-7; 6:1) As a Lion, He will close the books of history by His sovereign judgment upon it.

The veil over the Book has been lifted. Believers are given permission to understand its contents. It is a book accessible for our understanding.

Understanding the Book

There are the three simple keys to unlock this book - Symbolism, Chronology and Unity.

First, there are symbols, allusions and images throughout this Book. The Appendices are provided for a brief explanation of those symbolisms and images.

Second, the timetable for the Book of Revelation is basically chronological and in sequential order. (See Appendix I, Chart of Revelation)

Third, the Book of Revelation unites the Old and New Testaments. Of the 404 verses in the book of Revelation, 278 are taken from the Old Testament.[1] (See Appendix II, The OT in the NT.)

Though Revelation is approached as a simple book to understand, the final test will be in what actually happens in history. The proof of the accuracy of any prophetic interpretation will be found in its fulfillment.

[1] Kevin J Conner, Interpreting the Book of Revelation, (Portland, OR: Bible Temple Publishing, 1995) p. 33.

CHAPTER TWO

"I Wonder If There's a Purpose for Prophecy Being Revealed?"
JESUS AND HIS CHURCH

Summary: This Book's primary purpose is to reveal the Grandeur of Jesus, His plan for His church and His Sovereign control over the events of the coming global judgments.

Revelation One

An Introduction to the Book of Revelation

The opening statement says it all: "A Revelation of Jesus Christ."(1:1)

Although prophecies of judgment dominate the pages of this Book, its primary purpose is to declare who Jesus Christ really is.

In this book, Jesus is revealed both as a Lamb and a Lion.

First, He is revealed as a loving Lamb of grace and forgiveness to those who receive and love Him. Because He was crucified to free them from their selfish natures, believers will be transformed into God's image as "kings and priests."(1:5,6) We see these believers standing before the throne of God in worship and awe. (5:13; 19:1)

Second, He is revealed as a powerful Lion of judgment and wrath to those who reject His gift of love and forgiveness. They also stand before God's throne. But they will be sentenced to eternal judgment in the day of the resurrection of the ungodly. (20:12-14)

In this Book, we will see the final climax of history in the ultimate judgment of every person who has lived on earth. The eternal destiny of every person will be decided by the choice each has made. The ungodly will face Jesus as their Lion-Judge. The spirit of anarchy and rebellion will have no place in the coming kingdom of God and be eternally dealt with.

The horrendous judgments we will witness in this book are only a fraction of the eternal judgment that ultimately awaits the ungodly in the lake of fire and brimstone. (Revelation 20:10-15)

In Chapter One, we also see the nature of Jesus Christ revealed in symbolic form through the garments that cloth Him. (Revelation 1:12-16) He is standing in the middle of His church, described as the seven golden candlesticks. (Revelation 1:20) Jesus and His church are the focal point of the book of Revelation, not the judgments described in the book.

In Revelation Chapter One we encounter symbolic images of the Tabernacle of Moses and the High Priest order for the first time. These are the initial introduction to images borrowed from the Old Testament.[1] (Exodus 25:8,9; 31-40; 27:21-28:4) (See Appendix IV for The Tabernacle of Moses.)

Throughout this book, we will see images of pieces of furniture and the sacred rooms of the Tabernacle of Moses. We will also see the Feasts of Israel and the ten plagues of Egypt used as templates of prophetic images of things to come.

From Chapter One, we are introduced to Revelation as a book of symbols.

A promised blessing awaits those who read this book. (Revelation 1:3) No other book gives such a promise. Even if read out of simple obedience, the awesomeness of our Sovereign Lord will open the believer's hearts to the eternal and all-encompassing power and love of our Almighty Jesus. God's blessing awaits those who study this book.

[1]Debating Christianity & Religion, "Measuring the Tabernacle" <http://debatingchristianity.com/forum/viewtopic.php?p=358253>

CHAPTER THREE

"I Wonder If Churches Should be Interested in this Book?"

THE SEVEN CHURCHES

Summary: Jesus speaks to the unique needs of His church, commending, correcting and calling His church to a higher place of worship and service.

Revelation Two & Three

The 7 Churches Addressed By the Spirit

The Holy Spirit speaks to these seven churches (2:7,11,17,29; 3:6,13,22) but, specifically, to the angel of the churches. (2:1,8,12,18; 3:1,7,14) The angel of the church represents the messenger or leader of the church. Each of the seven churches is unique in setting, character, ministry and message from the Lord.

As we study each church, we will notice different facets of Jesus' nature that were revealed to us in Chapter One. One particular facet of Jesus' nature is uniquely connected to each of the seven different churches. Each part of His nature deals with the specific challenges that each church faces and gives instructions to meet those challenges.

For example, the Smyrna church is given the revelation of Jesus Christ as "the First and the Last, who was dead and came to life" (1:5,11; 2:8) to meet their unique challenge in facing suffering, persecution and martyrdom. (2:10,11)

In concert, each message to the seven churches contains (1) a compliment, (2) a correction for the church's sin, (except for the 2nd and 6th churches, which records no sins), (3) a call to contrition and (4) a promised compensation.

The churches can be seen from three major perspectives: 1) as historic, existing in the time of John and needing a message from the Lord about its strengths and weaknesses, 2) as representative of the seven phases of the church age from the first century to the current 21st century (from this perspective, we see ourselves living in the Philadelphia and Laodicea ages) and 3) as seven different types of local and global churches existing in the world today.[1]

The insights into these seven churches can assist the 21st century church to better understand itself. If these seven churches describe seven different types of churches that existed through all periods of history, then the Lord has given us a basis for evaluating every church in existence today. If each church today identifies with its matching 1st century church, then churches can receive a personal word of unique instruction from the Lord Jesus Himself.

These chapters can be approached historically and practically for every local and global church in the world today. These instructions are designed to prepare the church for its eternal destiny as it faces the coming judgment on the ungodly described in the following chapters.

[1] For further study, see these following websites:
http://en.wikipedia.org/wiki/Seven_churches_of_Asia
http://www.gotquestions.org/seven-churches-Revelation.html
http://mikebickle.org/resources/series/the-seven-churches-of-revelation
http://bridalcovenant.com/summary.html

CHAPTER FOUR

"I Wonder If God Sovereignly Controls the Events of History?"

HEAVEN AND JESUS CHRIST

Summary: Heaven's community worships the Lamb of God in His role as the Lion-Judge, watching as He unseals and is in total control of all the events of the coming global judgments.

Revelation Four & Five

A Vision of Heaven

In these chapters, we receive an amazing vision of heaven. It is focused on God sitting on His throne and multitudes of angels and the redeemed gathered around that throne. (4:2-3) We also observe that Jesus is the central focus of all of heaven as He administers the final day events.

Around God's eternal throne, we also see twenty-four elders seated on their thrones. These twenty-four elders seem to signify the leaders of the twelve tribes of Israel and the twelve apostles of the Lamb. They are key chosen leaders from the Old and New Testament. The twenty-four elders are part of the worshipping redeemed community of heaven. (4:4-11) These leaders might refer to actual individuals or the collective leadership from both the Old and New Testaments.

Also around the throne are four living creatures that depict the nature, life and ministry of Jesus Christ. The four description of those creatures as lion, calf, man and eagle reflect Jesus' nature discovered in the four gospels. They are also part of the worship community of heaven. (4:6-11; Ezekiel 1:4-10) Again, they could refer to actual individuals or represent collective believers from both testament periods. This description seems to indicate that redeemed individuals have matured into the image of Jesus: some as an authoritative roaring lion; others as a humble, serving calf; still others as an empathetic, compassionate person; and finally, some as a heaven-inspired, heaven-focused eagle.

The scrolls of judgments sealed since Daniel's day are in the hands of the Father. (5:1) All of heaven waits anxiously for someone worthy enough to break the seals that will unfold the events of the future. (5:2-4) John's heart is grieved, as no one is found worthy to open the seals.

Then, a Worthy One appears to break open the seven seals, one seal at a time. The Lion-King is announced "Worthy" to open the seals of judgment. Then, all of heaven expecting an enthroned King sees, instead, the unexpected - the scene of a wounded and broken Lamb. Awestruck in amazement, heaven sings a new song of worship to this Exalted Lamb. And He is none other than Jesus Christ, God's Son.

This reference of Jesus as the Lamb is more prominent than any other title He is given in this book. He is called the Lamb twenty-seven times in contrast to being entitled King only four times. Judgment on the earth proceeds out of His heart as a Lamb of love, not out of His life as an authoritative Lion-King.

The unveiling of Jesus the Lamb-King is about to take place. Redeemed human beings elevated to rule with their Lamb-King are also visible. (5:5-7) Billions of people from nations of the world who have received Jesus' gift of redemption and righteousness flood the royal court and stand around the throne of God worshipping Him. (5:9,10)

Multiple millions of angels also flock around the throne in worship of God. (5:11,12) Heaven resounds with deafening voluminous worship, as the climax of the ages is about to unfold.

This scene thrusts us into the future when every knee will bow and every tongue confesses that Jesus Christ is Lord. (5:13)

CHAPTER FIVE

"I Wonder If Today's Global Crises are Described in this Book?"

THE 7-SEALED JUDGMENTS

Summary: Jesus as a just Lamb-Judge begins to unseal and release a series of seven judgments paralleling the prophecy He gave in Matthew 24:6-8.

Revelation Six

Jesus begins to open the 7-Sealed Judgments. (Revelation 6:1)

We immediately see Jesus as the Lamb, the One who lovingly sacrificed His life for this world. It was of Him that John the Baptist proclaimed, He is "the Lamb of God that takes away the sins of the world."

Jesus is executing judgment as a Lamb, not a Lion.

The only one worthy of executing judgment on the world is the One who wholly loved it and gave His life for it. He is the only one who can justly close the book of history.

Almost 2,000 years ago, the Lamb-Redeemer, who declared the "acceptable year of the Lord" for three and a half years through His loving ministry, now pronounces the beginning of the final "day of the vengeance of our God" (Isaiah 61:1,2) as a Lion-Judge.

The Savior, who lovingly gave His life for the world, now enforces upon those who've rejected His love the just reward for their sins. It is no longer their sin that releases God's judgment but the act of their rejection of the forgiveness offered them. Those who have rejected His love are now exposed to the wrath they justly deserve by their choice.

Unsealing the Seven Sealed Judgments (See Appendix I, Chart))

Three sets of seven judgments begin to unfold from this point. Each set of these seven are separate and unique. They are opened sequentially in an orderly and purposeful manner, so the events must be taken as chronological in nature. Each has a different starting point and continues concurrently to expand in its impact until all the judgments are unfolded. They crescendo together leading to an explosive finale.

The following are the first seven:

The 1st Seal (6:2) discloses a rider on a white horse representing a Conquering King. White in the Bible consistently represents righteousness and holiness. This chapter presents Jesus, the Conquering King, rallying His army of followers to unite globally. This image seems to represent the church's powerful momentum over the past few centuries beginning from the Protestant Reformation to the Pentecostal/Charismatic movements. Today this movement accounts for almost one fifth of the world's population or 1.3 billion people on earth. This White Horseman appears again in Revelation 19 to finalize His conquest in His 2nd Coming. (19:11-16) The gospel has encircled the world fulfilling Jesus' prophecy in Matthew 24:14, "And this gospel of the kingdom will be preached to all the world as a witness to all the nations and then the end will come."

The 2nd Seal (6:3,4) releases a red horse that signifies global warfare between major nations, which parallels Jesus' prophecy of history's final days. (Matthew 24:3,7,8) Red represents bloodshed, the result of war. The greatest bloodshed in global history occurred in the past century. The fatalities of World War I totaled 10 million. World War II fatalities were mind-boggling, with over 55 million killed[1]! Revelation 9 predicts World War III as the most devastating of all wars, where a third of the earth's population will be destroyed. The following seals describe the other signs Jesus listed in Matthew 24. The wars of nations will multiply the current financial pressures on this world's already distressed and fragile economies. (See Appendix III, Matthew 24 and Revelation.)

The 3rd Seal (6:5,6) introduces a black horse into the world scene. Black is the color for darkness and depression, and presents a scene of economic chaos and famine. (Matthew 24:3,7,8) In 2010, the United Nations Food and Agriculture Organization estimated 950 million malnourished people or 1 of 7 in the world today.[2] Famines and economic chaos will accelerate worldwide. Hyperinflation will cause a loaf of bread to sell for a full day's wage, which amounts to an equivalent of $100 in today's US economy. John also sees an unequal distribution of wealth with the rich least affected by this inflationary trend. The Bible states that the rich will possess luxuries ("wine and oil"). If nations already face desperate economic and famine conditions, then imagine what it will be like after a major global conflict where weapons of mass destruction, germ warfare and atomic and nuclear power are unleashed.

The 4th Seal (6:7,8) releases a pale horse, which represents lack of color and life. John interprets this horse as signifying death, the terrible result of the 2nd and 3rd seals of war and famine. A pandemic of death sweeps the world in uncontrollable proportions. We have already seen fatalities of war and the extent of famine worldwide. Jesus explains this seal with the word, "pestilences" or epidemics and plagues. (Matthew 24:3,7,8) History bears out this prophecy of Jesus. The last two millenniums have seen the Smallpox Plague take 5 million lives in Rome in 165 AD, the Black Death take 100 million lives in Europe and Asia in 1338 AD, a Cholera Pandemic take one million lives in Russia in 1852 AD, the worldwide Flu Pandemic take 75 million lives in 1918 and the global HIV/AIDS epidemic affect 25 million from 1981 till now.[2] These events demonstrate the corruption and brokenness of this fallen world and its consequences, but in Jesus' own words, these are only the beginning of sorrows. ("Sorrows"= birth pangs, "Odin", Greek) These events are announcement of the coming new world of God's kingdom on earth. (21:1)

The 5th Seal (Revelation 6:9-11) reveals a time of great spiritual and religious persecution that has occurred throughout church history and will accelerate as the curtain of history falls. Jesus' words indicate that a characteristic feature of the end time will be the persecution of the elect. These seals are in alignment with Jesus' teachings of the last days. (Matthew 24:9-10)

Many will be martyred and the earth will be cursed with their blood crying out for vengeance. Justice must be served on an earth spilling the blood of innocent multitudes.

It is claimed that the 20th century persecutions were the most severe in the history of the church. According to the World Christian Encyclopedia (2001), some 45.4 million Christians were martyred in the 20th century. Other statistics show martyrdoms increasing yearly, from 35,000 in 1900, to 171,000 in 2005 to an estimated 260,000 in 2008.[3]

Jesus said that men would kill believers thinking they are doing God a service. (John 16.2) This happened in the Catholic Inquisition and is happening today under Islamic influence. The significant point in Matthew 24:9 is the hatred of Christians by all nations. That will include the westernized nations such as the USA, Canada, Europe, Australia etc.[4] It seems, from these passages, that the church must be prepared for persecution, not a rapture to avoid it.

This explanation from Scriptures and world events places the church and the nations at a place in history between the 5th and 6th seals. Every previous seal that the Lamb has opened will continue to accelerate in momentum and reach a climactic explosive finale leading to the 2nd Coming of Jesus in Revelation 19 to be studied later.

The 6th Seal (6:12-17) describes a life-threatening and terrifying scene that would be uncontrollable by human or governmental powers. All of man's wisdom and technology will stand helpless as nature's powers on earth and in the heavens unravel. This is what Jesus predicted before His return. Jesus said that "the sun will be darkened, and the moon will not give its light; the stars will fall from heaven" (Matthew 24:29) Jesus' description parallels the opening of this 6th seal where "the sun became black ... the moon became like blood and the stars of heaven fell to the earth..." (Revelation 6:12,13) Jesus sees this time when the "signs in the sun, and in the moon and in the stars" will cause "men's heart failing them from fear." (Revelation 6:14-17)(Luke 21:25,26)

We have already witnessed the unbridled powers of nature wreaking horrendous devastation through typhoons, hurricanes, tsunamis and earthquakes. Hundreds of thousands of lives have been taken. That is the result of the shaking of the powers of the earth.

How much more devastating will the results be when the power of the heavens begin to shake?

[1] Compare Anything, "World War I vs. World War II", <www.diffen.com/difference>

[2] Hunger Notes,"2012 World Hunger and Poverty Facts and Statistics", <www.worldhunger.org/articles>

[3] Wikipedia, "List of Epidemics", <http://en.wikipedia.org/wiki/List_of_epidemics>

[4.] Seeking Truth, "Persecution - Future", <http://www.seekingtruth.co.uk/persecution.htm>

CHAPTER SIX

"I Wonder If I can Know What will Happen to Believers?"

THE PROTECTION OF BELIEVERS

Summary: Jesus will protect His church from nature's destruction intended for the ungodly, but some believers must be ready to be martyred for their faith.

Amidst the scene of terrifying judgments resulting in desperate anxiety and fear, God promises His protection will be available to His people. But there will be some believers that will be asked to give their lives for Christ.

Revelation Six, Seven & Eight

The Sealed Believers (Revelation 7:1-8) clearly refer to the twelve tribes of Israel. They are the ones highlighted in this chapter. These twelve tribes are an image of the church of Jesus Christ.

The twelve tribes are called the "church in the wilderness." (Acts 7:38) They are the "seed of Abraham." (Galatians 3:29) The New Testament definitively uses the twelve tribes and Abraham's seed to point to God's spiritual Israel, the body of Christ and His church on earth.

The number 144,000 that is used here is also another allusion to the Church. That number was first mentioned in the Scripture in the structure of David's government during his reign as king of Israel. The number 144,000 is used frequently under David's leadership. This number also represents the church. (See Appendix VI, Bible Numeric)

These present a picture of those who are supernaturally protected from the devastation of these terrifying events. Fear will naturally grip human hearts. But the church will rest in supernatural peace amidst this chaotic period of history.

As Israel was protected and provided for when the 10 plagues assaulted Egypt and her idols, so God will preserve His church while nations and nature unravel. God's judgments will be directed at the ungodly world system, not against His people. Jesus already took God's judgment upon the cross. Just as God provided protection for Israel, so God will provide for His church.

Although believers will be shielded from upcoming disasters, they will not be immune from the worldwide persecution against the church. The ungodly, pricked in conscience by the godly lives of true believers, will react by attacking believers. All nations will hate them. (Matthew 24:9)

The Martyred Believers (Revelation 6:12-17) are pictured from all around the world encircling the throne room of God and worshipping with the four living creatures and the twenty-four elders. The time of great tribulation has begun and the church will experience being protected or martyred according to God's destiny and will.

The Seven Seal judgment predicts the emergence of a powerful church that will be protected from the judgment to come because they have accepted Jesus Christ who bore judgment in their place. It also describes a judgment upon ungodly men and systems amidst great Christian martyrdom.

Finally, the 7th Seal (Revelation 8:1-6) is opened. A calm before the explosive storm of the next seven series of judgments, which are the seven trumpets, sets in. These scenes are chronological in nature because the seven trumpets emerge out of the seventh of the seven seal judgments.

If you remember in Revelation 1:12,20, we saw Jesus, as a High Priest, standing in the midst of the seven golden candlesticks that were positioned closest to the Outer Court in Moses' Tabernacle.

In contrast, we see a High Priest stand before the incense altar, (Exodus 25:1-30:38) closest to the Holy of Holies (the place of God's sacred presence on the earth). This scene describes a time in history "Before" but not quite yet "In" the Holy of Holies. (See Appendix IV, Tabernacle of Moses.)

The High Priest ministering with a censer and incense rising up before God only takes place on the Day of Atonement. (Leviticus 16:1-34) This Day was part of the Feast of Tabernacles that took place once a year. The High Priest was allowed into the Holy of Holies only on that one day to atone for the nation's sin (Leviticus 23:1-44; Deuteronomy 16:1-17) and, because of that day, Israel would have its sins covered until the following year's Day of Atonement.

This event in the book of Revelation seems to point to the fulfillment of the Day of Atonement for the church. As the Passover and Pentecost Feasts were fulfilled in the life of the church, the feast of Tabernacles and the Day of Atonement will be fulfilled. These events draw us closer into the throne room of God and prepare us for the climax of God's final purposes on earth. (See Appendix V, Feasts of Israel.)

Maintaining the picture of the Feasts of Israel, the next set of judgments reflects another feast called the Feast of Trumpets. The Feast of Trumpets was used to unite Israel for major instructions in directions and activities. The trumpet was used to call leaders to unite, journeys to begin and battles to be fought. (Numbers 10:1-10)

The next series of judgments are called the Trumpet Judgments and they go beyond the judgment of the ungodly. These judgments also give direction to the believer for the next dimension of God's purpose of bringing His kingdom to this earth.

CHAPTER SEVEN

"I Wonder If Earth's History is Predicted in this Book?"

THE 7-TRUMPET JUDGMENTS

Summary: The Seven Trumpet Judgments emerge out of the 7th Seal and devastate earth's natural resources and predict the coming World War III.

Revelation Eight, Nine & Ten

The Blowing of the Seven Trumpet Judgments

This next set of Trumpet judgments appears to be a series of judgments distinct in nature from the first Seven Seal Judgments. The first seven focused on the growth of the church and the judgment on nations, religious ideologies and economies.

This second series of judgments focuses on the physical planet earth itself, utilizing natural and unnatural phenomena and powerful spiritual forces of darkness rising in dominance on the earth. This set of judgments seems to emerge out of the 6th seal and unravels the natural powers of earth and heavens. What was begun in the 6th seal accelerates into major cataclysmic events depicted in these seven trumpet judgments.

What is released in these next seven judgments combine what is reminiscent of Joshua's march around Jericho and the Exodus of Israel.

In Joshua's march, seven trumpets of judgments were blown for seven days that brought judgment upon the strongest fortress in Canaan. This opened the door to the conquest of the entire land of Canaan. This is similar to what God will do in the final seven trumpets of Revelation.

These trumpets are also reminiscent of the time of the Exodus. Israel broke free from Egyptian domination under the leadership of Moses. The plagues released on Egypt polluted water systems, unleashed hail and fire, turned water to blood, killed fish life, diseased bodies, released locusts, destroyed agriculture and darkened the earth.[1] (See Appendix VII, The 10 Plagues of Egypt.)

Similar plagues as against Egypt are hurled upon unbelieving mankind during this set of judgments. The plagues in Egypt assaulted the false gods of the Egyptians and proclaimed the LORD God as the only one God of the earth. That same lesson will be learned through these seven trumpet judgments. God's purpose is to reveal the instability of these world's gods and direct the world's attention to the unchanging God of creation, history and salvation.

As in Egypt in Moses' day, the purpose of God in the 10 plagues was not to punish His people, but to set the stage for their release to the Promised Land. When Israel was released in the Exodus, they were led through the wilderness and eventually experienced military dominance over all nations of the world.

God will do a similar thing for His church through these trumpet judgments. The church will be released of its bondages, survive their wilderness and will be established in leadership over all nations of the world at the return of Jesus.

Along with preparing His people for new life, God will turn the hearts of many to Himself, as took place in Egypt. When Israel was released from their Egyptian captivity, many Egyptian families left the land of Egypt with them. These judgments prepared the believer but also opened the hearts of the unbelievers as well.

These set of judgments go beyond what is recorded of Israel's experience in Egypt. We also see a multiplied intensity and a greater shaking of the powers of the heavens than the events in the 6th Seal. Gigantic volcanoes erupting, large asteroids crashing on the earth, lights of heaven turning dark, stars falling and nations at war utilizing unimaginable weaponry of destruction become a global phenomenon.

Here is the order in which the trumpets are blown and the events take place:

The 1st Trumpet (8:7) unleashes hail, fire and blood and a third of the trees and all the green grass on the entire earth are burnt.

The 2nd Trumpet (8:8,9) describes a great mountain exploding with fire, thrown into the sea, a third of the sea turns to blood, a third of sea life dies and a third of the world's ship destroyed. From this description, it seems that a gigantic volcanic eruption or multiple gigantic eruptions explode across the planet.

The 3rd Trumpet (8:10,11) sounds and a large star (or asteroid) falls from heaven and a third of the sea and rivers are affected with poisonous pollutants.

The 4th Trumpet (8:12,13) sounds and the powers of the heavenly bodies – the sun, moon and stars – are affected. A third of light fails to shine. This seems like such a disastrous event, but an angel announces that even greater sorrows are ready to burst on the scene of the world.

The 5th Trumpet (9:1-12) sounds and another star falls on earth to release spiritual powers, like locusts, that bring more death and devastation on the earth. Men will seek to die, but cannot. Locust in the Bible represents God's judgment on people and agricultural products when lives are lived apart from obedience to His will and Word.

The 6th Trumpet (9:13-21) releases demonic powers resident in the region of the Euphrates River, originating in today's Turkey and flowing through Syria and Iraq, mobilizing an army of 200,000,000 soldiers from the east to invade and conquer the world. These military powers seem to unleash epidemics and plagues that might indicate the possibility of germ warfare resulting in a third of mankind killed. This trumpet suggests that World War III is on the horizon of the world scene.

The 7th Trumpet (10:7) sounding seems to introduce a unique period of time on the earth. This trumpet has a beginning, no immediate end, and a continuing influence for a specified period of time – "in the *days* of the *sounding* of the 7th angel". A special set of "seven thunders", unexplained and mysteriously sealed, is released prior to the last trumpet sounding. (10:1-6) The 7th Trumpet's blast seems to introduce what follows in Revelation 11-13 and 14-19.

[1] Wikipedia, "Plagues of Egypt", <http://en.wikipedia.org/wiki/Plagues_of_Egypt>

CHAPTER EIGHT

"I Wonder If I'll Recognize the Major Last Day Events?"

THE 3.5 YEARS OF GREAT TRIBULATION

Summary: The 7th Trumpet is sounded. God's final 3.5-year plan is described. God's two witnesses (Chapter 11), the woman, Satan & man-child (Chapter 12) and the Anti-Christ world system (Chapter 13) emerge. The return of Jesus Christ to earth is being paved.

The 7th Trumpet signals a unique period in earth's history that most Bible scholars call the period of Great Tribulation. The events of the next three chapters interconnect the prophecies found in the twin prophetic books of Daniel and Revelation. (See Appendix VIII & IX, 70-Week Prophecy and Daniel & Revelation.)

Revelation Eleven, Twelve & Thirteen

The next three chapters describe three major tribulation events.

1) Chapter 11 records the emergence of two powerful witnesses for Christ that is reminiscent of Moses and Elijah of the Old Testament.

2) Chapter 12 presents the mysterious birth of a Christ-like creation through the Bride of Christ, the church.

3) Chapter 13 predicts the rise of the anti-Christ's system through a ten-nation coalition.

In an objective reading of Revelation 11-13, we clearly see only one specific time period mentioned five times. (11:2,3; 12:6,14; 13:5) Only a 3.5-year period is mentioned. No reference is made of a 7-year period. The only reasonable conclusion anyone can arrive at is that a 3.5 year tribulation period is being described in chapters 11-13, not a 7-year period.

[Note: Another approach to this 3.5-year period is the study of Daniel's 70 Week Prophecy. (See Appendix VIII, 70-Week Prophecy) According to Daniel's prophecy, Jesus fulfilled the first 3.5 years in His earthly ministry. Therefore an elusive final 3.5-year period remains to be discovered. That 3.5 years is unveiled in Revelation 11-13.]

The obvious conclusion is that all three chapters are taking place in the same 3.5-year period. They describe separate but parallel events occurring at the same time. The following are a brief description of those chapters.

The Three and a Half Year Worldwide Events

The Two Witnesses - Revelation 11 describes the powerful clash between God's messengers on earth and the powers of evil ruling the world during this time. These two witnesses emerge on the world scene at the beginning of the 3.5-year tribulation period. The true identity of these two witnesses will only be known as the future events unfold.

Currently, we can only speculate that they are either two men similar in ministry to (if not actually) Moses and Elijah themselves (11:5,6) or they could be two groups of God's people given a powerful ministry that is manifesting the gifts of miracles and power displayed by Moses and Elijah. If they are individuals they will be located in physical Jerusalem. Or if they represent a group of global ministries, they will be scattered worldwide, working with the body of Christ.

Either way they will parallel Jesus' death and be killed at the end of the 3.5-year period as Jesus was. Worldwide media broadcast will capture this event and, within 3.5 days, the entire world will see them miraculously resurrect from the dead like Jesus Christ did. This event will be broadcasted across the world, and people will be stunned into the fear of God. (11:7-11)

The grand finale of this 3.5-year period culminates with three significant events:

(1) The 7th angel's crescendo blast that will coincide with the ascension of the two witnesses and parallel Jesus' ascension to heaven, [This could also possibly parallel the rapture of believers at the 2nd Coming.]

(2) The Lord's Prayer, "Your kingdom come. Your will be done on earth on earth as it is in heaven," will become a reality, (11:12,15) (Matthew 6:10) and

(3)"God's glory will fill the earth as the waters cover the sea." (Numbers 14:21; Habakkuk 2:14) History will step into the presence of God. The Ark of the Covenant is seen for the first time.

The Ark symbolizes the resting place of God's glorious presence in the Tabernacles of Moses. (11:19) (See Appendix IV, Tabernacle of Moses.) This also symbolizes the annual ceremony of the Day of Atonement when the High Priest goes in the Holy of Holies and the nation's sins are covered. (See Appendix V, Feast of Israel.) This is also part of the Feast of Tabernacles, the time of harvest celebration for Israel. (See Chapter Nine, Two Global Harvests, Page 40,41.)

The Woman, Man-child & Dragon - Revelation 12 describes the supernatural birth of a man-child by a woman. Because the final 3.5 years of Daniel 9 is mentioned twice in this chapter (Revelation 12:6,14), this event should be viewed more prophetic than historic. [Some Bible teachers see this as a historic event of the birth of Jesus Christ, not a prophetic event of the future.]

Taken prophetically, this woman represents the bride of Christ. This bride gives birth to a supernatural man-child. The man-child's birth seems to have all the characteristics of the birth of Jesus Christ 2,000 years ago. It is also associated with Satan's attempts to take His life. (12:1-4; Matthew 2:16)

If the woman who births this man-child represents a corporate group or the bride of Christ, the church, then it seems logical to assume that this child will also represent a company of people.

This man-child will fulfill God's original purpose for Adam who was declared to have dominion over and subdue the earth.

This child is pictured to rule the nations of the earth. But, at the same time, the dragon will assault the woman, who will be preserved in the wilderness by God, reflective of Israel being preserved in her forty years of wilderness wandering. (12:5,6)

The Anti-Christ & False Prophet - Revelation 13 records the emergence of the anti-Christ on the earth. Like the two witnesses and woman and man-child, the anti-Christ's activities will be confined to a brief 3.5-year period. The anti-Christ will be allowed to rule the world. He will blaspheme God and lead nations to persecute and overcome believers. (13:6-8) His power will arise out of a conglomerate of 10-17 nations and he will have the reputation of possessing supernatural power. (13:1,3,13) The entire world system will be united together to honor and worship him. (13:3,4,12)

Our current global economy seems desperate enough to embrace a person or system like this anti-Christ. The economic debt crisis in Europe and the out-of-control budget crisis in the United States could lead the world to tighten control on the financial systems of nations very soon. A person or nation that could provide a miraculous solution to alleviate the coming financial Armageddon would be hailed as the global leader. This would pave the way for the emergence of an anti-Christ system. John sees this anti-Christ controlling the world's financial purse strings and having the power to determine who can buy or sell in the newly established world economy. (13:16) He also sees that the number 666 will be connected to its identity. (13:18)

These Events are Time Markers

God has left these three events as prophetic time markers. They will mark the final days of tribulation and the preparation for the 2nd Coming of Jesus Christ.

Though we will not know exactly the "day nor the hour that the Son of Man will return," (Matthew 24:36) believers are not left in "darkness" and ignorant of the final days of history. The

Bible is clear that believers will know the "times and the seasons." (I Thessalonians 5:1,4,5)

So, though believers will not know precisely the "day nor the hour" that Jesus Christ will return, they will know the general vicinity of time when He will return.

Clearly from the events of these chapters, believers should know the return of Jesus Christ to earth within a space of 3.5 years. (See Appendix XI, The 2nd Coming of Christ.)

CHAPTER NINE

"I Wonder If The Worldwide Harvest has been Predicted?"

TWO GLOBAL HARVESTS

Summary: Two harvests of souls are found in this chapter: 1) a harvest of the ungodly to face the wrath of God and 2) a harvest of the godly leading to eternal life.

Revelation Fourteen

We are living in historic times for the church and the world.

A worldwide spiritual harvest predicted by the prophets is taking place today. An abundant harvest of souls is being reaped across the nations of this world.

Jesus taught that the end of the age would be characterized by a harvest of both good and evil. (Matthew 13:36-50) This harvest theme fulfills the progressive prophetic imagery of the Feasts of Israel, spotlighting the final Feast of Tabernacles, the harvest feast. (See Appendix V, The Feasts of Israel.)

The church has grown from 120 disciples in its inception to a population of 1 out of over 300 persons or 1/3 of 1% by the end of the first century. Today, 2 of 7 billion or almost 1/3 of the world embrace Jesus as Messiah, and the numbers keep growing. The Roman Catholics are the largest group with a billion persons. The Protestant Movement number about 800 million and the Orthodox Church has about 260 million members. In the US, approximately 79% of the population consider themselves Christians.[1]

But even as God's Spirit is at work, so are the powers of darkness. They realize their time is short. In this chapter we see two harvests taking place together - an abundant harvest of souls for God's kingdom and an opposing harvest of evil motivated by satanic powers.

Revelation 14 describes one harvest that will enlarge God's kingdom and church in the world. The other will bring judgment on the ungodly possessed by the dictates of darkness and the anti-Christ system on the earth.

As we near the time of the end, these two harvests will clash more intensely in ideology, value and lifestyle. Evil will grow more corrupt and righteousness will grow more brightly.

The Bible is clear: God's glorious light will shine at a time of gross darkness. (Isaiah 60:2)

The Harvest of Wrath

The entire book of Revelation records God's judgment upon the ungodly on the earth. Revelation 14:8-11,17-20 explains this judgment through the image of a harvest that will grow in numbers and culminate in the historic battle of Jesus Christ with the opposing military forces of this world called Armageddon. (19:11-21)

The Harvest of Godly Souls

God will also reap a harvest of people committed to godliness and righteousness on the earth. They are described as worshippers. (14:2,3) They have a heart like their Father God. (14:1,4) And they will follow Him completely.(14:4) An end-time revival will take place with the reaping of multitudes of lost souls into His kingdom. (14:14-16) This is the fulfillment of Jesus' instruction to pray for a fruitful harvest (Matthew 9:38,39) and the ultimate promise that the gospel will be preached to all nations before the time of the end. (Matthew 24:14) Church statisticians can confirm that this prophecy is now being fulfilled on the earth.

[1] http://christianity.about.com/od/denominations/p/christiantoday.htm

CHAPTER TEN

"I Wonder If Cataclysmic Events will Increase & Worsen?"

THE 7-VIAL JUDGMENTS

Summary: The final seven judgments will devastate the world and prepare God's people for Jesus' 2nd Coming and the Millennium Kingdom.

Revelation Fifteen & Sixteen

As the world draws nearer to the coming of Christ, the contrast between light and darkness, good and evil will be magnified. Evil, corruption and wickedness will become an acceptable lifestyle as never before. Selfishness and greed will dominate human hearts in education, business and government. God and His people will be systematically shut out of the world's system but miraculously provided for by the Lord.

God's purpose is to restore the fallen earth and bring humankind back to His original plan from the Garden of Eden. But, because the earth and the universe has been corrupted by sin, then all of mankind and creation must undergo a cleansing process to prepare for a major transformation into a "new heaven and new earth." (21:1)

Chapter fifteen is a short introduction to the final and full wrath of God to be poured upon the earth. God's judgments climax in the following two chapters as the bowls or vials are being poured out. The "cloud of witnesses" (Hebrews 12:1), which are comprised of Old and New Testament believers, (15:3) surround the throne of God, anticipating the final act of history. Though evil and wickedness will be under assault and devastated by these vials, they are, nevertheless, still under the control of our Sovereign Lord.

God's temple is filled with His glory. This is a picture that is reflective of the completion of the Tabernacle of Moses and the Temple of Solomon in the Old Testament. In both events, the priests could not stand in the presence of God. As these events of judgment are about to take place, God is completing His plan on the earth. (Exodus 40:35; I Kings 8:10,11) God's promised glory will fill His people and the earth.

The Seven Vial Judgments (15:1,6,7) present God's final actions to destroy evil. The stage is set in heaven as the Holy of Holies is filled with the glory of God's presence that signifies our entrance into the final room of God's plan. We are faced with the Holy of Holies. It is the final step in God's purposes on the earth. (15:6,8)

These next series of judgment again parallel the judgment poured out upon Egypt to set God's people Israel free. But in contrast to Egypt these judgments will occur in a more forcefully magnified intensity and thrust God's people, the body of Christ, into their highest purpose.

This is the climax of God's judgment on the world that will end in the war of Armageddon, the 2nd coming of Christ, His millennial reign and the new heaven and earth. These seven-vial judgments are the necessary "birth pangs" of God's new creation life, similar to a butterfly emerging out of its cocoon from the life of a caterpillar. God's final purpose for man, earth and the universe will emerge from these judgments.

A brief description of the final seven bowl or vial judgments are listed: (See Appendix VII, The Plagues of Egypt.)

The 1st Vial Judgment (16:2) pours out a foul sore on men identified with the anti-Christ system of that day. This judgment is comparable to the 6th plague of Egypt, which were the incurable boils Egypt suffered. (Exodus 9:8-12)

The 2nd Vial Judgment (16:3) turns the sea into blood across the world and every living sea-life dies. In Moses' day, the first plague turned the Nile River that watered Egypt into blood, destroying all its river life. This 2nd bowl judgment will pollute the ocean systems across the earth.

The 3rd Vial Judgment (16:4) turns the rivers and springs of water into blood across the world. Egypt's 1st plague affected its Nile River system. This 3rd vial judgment will extend beyond the ocean and affect every source of water supply on the earth. All of earth's water supply will be polluted and turned into blood.

The Lord is worshipped as just and holy in executing these judgments because of the blood of innocent martyrs shed on the earth during this time. "God is not mocked. Whatsoever a man sows, even so shall he reap." (Galatians 6:7) "Do unto others as you would have done unto you." (Matthew 7:12)

The Lord is returning upon unrepentant and violent mankind their reward for the shedding of the innocent blood of the righteous.

The 4th Vial Judgment (16:8) scorches men with fire but, rather than turning to God for help, they refuse to honor God and instead, blaspheme Him even more. In the 7th plague of Egypt, fire appeared and scorched the ground after the thunder roared and hail fell. (Exodus 9:13-35)

In this 4th Vial judgment, the fire assaults people's bodies causing intense anguish, but results in no repentance or humility of heart. Human hearts are hardened against the Lord even as the Egyptian Pharaoh's heart was hardened against God in Moses' day.

The 5th Vial Judgment (16:10) turns the earth from light to darkness. The event of the 9th plague of Egypt is repeated in this final scene of history. (Exodus 10:21-29) But this event has a widespread impact. Darkness covers the earth as every source of light is taken from the earth. This physical darkness reflects the spiritual darkness dominating human hearts across the world.

What happened locally in the nation of Egypt will take place globally across the entire world. The prophet's declaration of how "Darkness will cover the earth" (Isaiah 60:1) will reflect the spiritual darkness that will engulf the ungodly on planet earth. This is the midnight darkness before the dawning of a new day.

The 6th Vial Judgment (16:12) is centered again on the Euphrates River. Demonic spirits are released and the kings of the earth gather their military might to contest the power of God.

This reminds us of Egypt's military chariots attempting to slaughter Israel as they fled across the Red Sea. But rather than slaughter Israel, God, through the waters of the Red Sea, devastated the ruling power of that day. The walls of the sea collapsed as Jericho's walls fell. The enemy was annihilated.

This bowl judgment describes a similar battle scene called the final war of Armageddon. (16:16) (See Appendix X, The War of Armageddon.)

The 7th Vial Judgment (16:17-21) describes the final blow to the Anti-Christ system as earthquakes topple cities, islands are submerged and mountains collapse. Seventy pounds hailstones pellet the earth and wreak havoc on properties and lives.

This, again, is reflective of the devastating result of the plagues against Egypt, but taking place in a greater intensity in these final days. Inconceivable destruction takes place across the world to finalize God's plan for the earth. As a mother in the final stage of her birth pangs and delivery of her baby, God's babies, His spiritual Israel, are emerging into their eternal and spiritual destiny.

CHAPTER ELEVEN

"I Wonder If the World's Systems will be Destroyed?"

GLOBAL JUDGMENT

Summary: The final days of the morally corrupt system called "Mother of Harlots" and the financially corrupt system called "Babylon" are targeted and judged.

Revelation Seventeen & Eighteen

The next two chapters describe the final state of the world as the last judgments are hurled upon it. These scenes describe the morally perverse lifestyle filling the earth in chapter 17. It also describes the economic corruption that will characterize nations and corporations across the world in chapter 18. They describe what life without God and His Biblical values will be like.

These events give a close-up snapshot of the last few days or final weeks of the 3.5-year period described in Revelation 11-13. These events also seem to coincide with the seven vials.

Judgment on the Morally Perverse

Chapter 17 describes the devastation coming upon the earth's population that accepts sexual perversion as normal. (17:15) The Anti-Christ system (17:3,12) is described as "the Mother of Harlots." It is full of abominations and filthy in its fornication. (17:4)

The rise of sex slave trading, homosexuality, accelerated experimental drugs and internet pornography will only grow increasing worse as we rush toward the time of the end. These morally perverse nations will develop a powerful military force that will marshal its might to war against the Lamb. (17:14)

The Russian war against Israel prophesied in Ezekiel 38-39 will take place during this time. (See Appendix X, The War of

Armageddon.) These events will culminate in the clash of forces leading to the 2nd coming of Jesus.

Judgment on the Monetarily Corrupt

The world is shaking from the impact of the 2008 derivative fiasco of the Wall Street mortgage brokers. That scheme has negatively shaken the world's bond markets and traumatized the entire American real estate industry.

Not only has moral perversion infiltrated the US and the world, but financial corruption has also polluted every nation today. That corruption will worsen in days ahead and influence every banking system of the world. (18:3)

This event will be like a modern day Tower of Babel. (Genesis 11:1ff) It is a financial system called "Babylon", an allusion reminding us of the Babel and Babylon of the Old Testament. (17:5; 18:2,10,21)

Advanced communication technology will lead to the jailbreak of language limitations that inhibited Babel's evil purposes. The world will be united, as in the days of Babel. The rise of English as the language of choice for communication globally will also advance this modern day Babel. But, as in the Babel of Genesis 11, the world's Babylonian system will be brought down and destroyed by the judgment of God.

Revelation announces Babylon's demise and devastation that will take place on one fateful day. (18:8,10,17) The book of Revelation shows how the financial markets across the world will collapse in a twenty-four hour period bringing great anguish and torment to the evil and corrupted traders across the world. (18:9-19)

Because the world today is interconnected in its economic system, what happens in one sector will affect all the other global sectors. We saw a preview of what is to come. What began before 2008 as a benign economic tremor turned overnight into a mind-shocking financial earthquake from which the global markets have yet to recover. What rocked the world economy in

2008 will pale in comparison to the financial markets shaken by God's judgment in the last days.

The intent of God through this judgment is to reveal the folly of the greed of materialism and for mankind to repent and return to Him. But, as we shall see, the stronghold of avarice will lead to further selfishness, destruction and judgment.

All of these events will lead to the final curtain call of history we will see described in the next few chapters.

CHAPTER TWELVE

"I Wonder If There will be an Armageddon?"
"I Wonder If There will be the 2nd Coming of Christ?"

ARMAGEDDON AND THE SECOND COMING

Summary: The war of Armageddon describes the final clash of the world's military forces against the power of the armies of Jesus Christ in His 2nd Coming.

Revelation Nineteen

The 2nd Coming of Christ is described only once in the book of Revelation. We find it here in Revelation 19. There are many attempts to impose the 2nd Coming into obscure verses in Revelation. But none is as obvious and definitive as what John saw in Chapter 19.

This event is climatic and visible. It is just as the angels declared it would be when Jesus ascended to heaven. (Acts 1:9-11) They did not say that the 2nd Coming is silent or secretive. There is no indication of a mysterious snatching up of believers to avoid the persecution and martyrdom other generations had to face for their testimony for Christ. (See Appendix XI, The 2nd Coming of Christ.)

As we have seen so far in this prophetic book, the church goes through the tribulation, faces persecution, declares the good news and is preserved to welcome Jesus at His return.

The 2nd Coming of Jesus Christ (Revelation 19)

This event will take place as the world system comes under judgment and a great harvest of souls will be reaped worldwide. (Matthew 24:14) Judgment will fall upon the morally perverse and financially corrupt of the world.

It seems that both heaven and earth will blend their voices to rejoice in anticipation of the final climax of human history. Heaven is looking expectantly for the completion of the bride of

Christ and the perfection of God's church. (19:1-10) God's created world is longing for release from the bondage of sin. This release will happen at Jesus' return. (Romans 8:19-21) The children of God will mature and develop into the very image of Christ because of Christ's redemption and the empowerment of the Spirit. (19:10)

Then, every eye will see Jesus Christ's return, including the Jewish nation that crucified Him. (1:7; Matthew 24:27-30) As Israel became a physical nation in May 14, 1948, they shall be born-again as a spiritual nation at the 2nd coming. (Isaiah 66:8)

No longer will Jesus be a lone rider. (6:2) He will now be leading an army of mature saints. He will be clothed in righteous garments and deliver the final judgment on those that have chosen the path of corruption and wickedness.

Under Joshua's leadership, God used Israel's army to destroy the nations of Canaan because wickedness was boiling and overflowing its caldron. God will likewise use Jesus and His army to evict the evil nations globally and a new kingdom will rule the nations with Jesus as King of Kings and as Lord of Lord. (19:11-21)

This is the final war of Armageddon. The kings of the earth will be defeated, the Anti-Christ captured and they and their followers judged for all eternity. God's plan of restoration is nearing its completion awaiting the rule of the only One that can govern righteously, fairly and compassionately on the earth. The long-awaited day of peace, joy and love has arrived! Jesus will sit on His throne to reign supreme on the earth!

CHAPTER THIRTEEN

"I Wonder If The World really will be Different?"

THE MILLENNIUM AND THE JUDGEMENT

Summary: A world government ruled by Christ for 1,000 years will be followed by a Great White Throne judgment.

Revelation Twenty

The Millennial Reign of Christ (Revelation 20:1-10)

The time after the 2nd Coming will see the establishing of the 1,000 years governmental rule of God and Jesus Christ on planet earth.

As the worship in Solomon's Temple and his reign over nations took center stage following the worship inspired in David's Tabernacle and David's rule as king over Israel, so the Millennial worship and reign of Christ and His dominance over nations will follow the worship and rule of Jesus Christ over His church during the previous two millennium.

Life as God intended mankind to live it will be demonstrated for a 1,000-year period. "Death will finally lose its sting; Grave will lose its victory!" Sickness, pain, disease, war and crime will be experiences of the past. (I Corinthians 15:55)

Satan will be bound in the bottomless pit during this time unable to influence nations or persons. The influence of the Holy Spirit alone will dominate planet earth during this period. Solomon's dominion of peace will be brought to earth again.

Those who lived for Christ will become joint-heirs with Him ruling over nations of the world. The resurrection of dead believers will have taken place at the 2nd coming of Christ. (I Thessalonians 4:13-18)

The unbelieving dead will remain in Hades and not be resurrected until the end of the 1,000-year period. At the end of that period, Satan will be released in one last desperate attempt to deceive the nations but will again be defeated and thrown into the lake of fire and brimstone forever.

The Great White Throne Judgment (Revelation 20:11-15)

This is not the judgment of believers because their judgment has already been absorbed in Jesus' sacrifice on the cross. (Acts 8:33) Adam's sin brought the judgment of death, but Jesus' gift brought justification and righteousness to believers. (Romans 5:16,18) For believers, this is not a day of trembling and fear, but one of boldness and thankfulness. (John 4:17)

This final judgment is the judgment of unbelievers, who have refused the judgment of God through Christ that believers in Jesus have received. (I Corinthians 11:31)

Like God's purpose in the judgment against Egypt to bring Pharaoh and that nation to repentance, God's intent throughout the Book of Revelation is to bring the ungodly to repentance. But those whose knees would not bow voluntarily to the Lordship of Christ before the White Throne judgment will be compelled to recognize His Lordship as that final day judgment will be issued.

Unbelievers will be judged based on how they lived their lives. Believers will not be judged based on their own records. The Lamb's Record of Life will replace the believer's record. There will be no question regarding the fairness of God in condemning those whose names are not found in the Lamb's Book of Life. Those condemned will be cast into the lake of fire along with Satan, the Anti-Christ and their followers.

CHAPTER FOURTEEN

"I Wonder If I can know what heaven will be like?"

THE NEW HEAVEN & NEW EARTH

Summary: The Lord's Prayer is finally answered. God's "kingdom has come on earth" and His people "conformed to the image of His Son." God's plan for the restoration of "the new heaven and new earth" is complete.

Revelation Twenty-One & Twenty-Two

A New Heaven & New Earth (Revelation 21:1)

God's plans have come full circle. The Lord initially created the first heaven and earth in Genesis 1:1. But it was marred by Adam's mistrust and sin, resulting in creation's fallen state. Since that time, God's plan of redemption and restoration has been sovereignly in motion. In these final chapters, we see His plan beautifully and graciously executed.

In Revelation 21:1, we see a time of new beginnings. God is now able to execute His original plan in the lives of His people as initially intended in Genesis 1.

Redemption is complete. A "New Heaven & New Earth" is created in perfection and is now unable to be marred by sin. The stage is now set for an uninterrupted fulfillment of God's plan. We have returned to the beginning.

After 7,000 years of recorded Bible history, the heaven and earth is now ready for what "eyes has not seen, nor ears heard, nor have entered into the heart of man, the things which God has prepared for those who love Him." (I Corinthians 2:9) What Jesus, God's Lamb, gave His life for will now be fully realized!

The New Jerusalem (Revelation 21:2-11)

The Bride of Christ is now complete and God and His people are united as one. His people will inherit the resources prepared for His children.

The kingdom of heaven has come to earth fulfilling the church's constant prayer, "Thy kingdom come, Thy will be done, on earth as it is in heaven." (Matthew 6:10)

Nations and their kings from around the world will follow and worship the Lord. (21:24)

Heaven will not be an ethereal concept in some distant location in the outer limits of our universe.

This chapter describes heaven as God's kingdom descending upon and residing on planet earth. Planet earth was designed to be the place where heaven would be experienced. What God originally planned for our first parents in Eden will finally materialize.

Heavenly Jerusalem will finally descend to earth and Jerusalem's walls, foundations and gates are described in detail. (21:12-21)

We will live in the presence of God's brilliant glory. There will be no need for the light of the sun because God Himself will provide the illumination for His kingdom on earth. (21:22-22:5) Israel saw the diminishing glory of God on the veiled face of Moses. We will see that glory in its unobstructed splendor in the unveiled face of the Father and His Son. Believers will bask in God's undiminished brilliance greater than the noonday sun and enjoy it forever.

Behold, I Come Quickly (Revelation 22:6-21)

What is prepared is far beyond comprehension! We are given a slight glimpse of what is to come by John's interaction with his guide. As his prophetic tour ends, John acknowledges his escort as His Master, Jesus Christ, and begins to honor Him.

He bows down to worship Him, but is astonished by these words, "Do not do this! I am a prophet as you are. Only worship God!" (22:8,9) This is the second time John made this mistake. The first was found in Revelation 19:10.

Why did John twice make this mistake of assuming a fellow prophet for His Master, Jesus Christ?

The answer to this question yields an amazing revelation of God's plan for humankind.

John couldn't believe what he saw. What he saw was the completion of God's indescribable plan. John saw the Revelation of Jesus Christ, the purpose initially stated for this book.

But it was the Revelation of Jesus Christ - not "To" His people, but "In" His people. God's children will be shaped into the image of Christ. They will become just like Jesus Christ. That is what John saw! Who John assumed was Jesus Christ was actually a fellow prophet whom he mistook for Jesus Christ!

Jesus gave His life as a seed sown by a farmer intending to reap a harvest. (John 12:24) All farmers know that a seed sown will multiply a harvest of similar seeds. But farmers only reap a harvest of fruits or vegetables. Jesus Christ will reap a harvest of people - believers just like Him.

Because of His sacrifice on the cross, believers in Christ will be "conformed to the image of His son" (Romans 8:29), "be like Him" (I John 3:2) and "fashioned like His glorious body." (Philippians 3:21)

How does a caterpillar turn into a butterfly or a coal into a beautiful, valuable diamond? It happens only by God's sovereign power. Believers will become what they were created to be. They were to be "made in the image of God" (Genesis 1:26,27)

"Beloved, now are we the sons of God, and we are not what we shall be, but we know that when He appears, we shall be like Him, for we shall see Him as He is." (I John 3:2)

Throughout this prophetic book, we have seen Jesus as the Lamb-Lion or Compassionate Judge. He, who became the sacrificial Lamb, is the Only One who could rightfully become the world's final Judge. 2,000 years of mercy in the "acceptable year of the Lord" has preceded these final days of just "vengeance of our God."

We have seen unveiled "The revelation of Jesus Christ" in His role as the Righteous Judge over the earth and the completion of God's restoration plan for all mankind.

But not only have we seen Jesus unveiled, we have seen what is awaiting believers in the final global harvest, His 2nd Coming, the millennium and God's kingdom coming to earth.

But beyond our wildest expectation, we have not only seen the unveiling of Jesus, our Lamb-Lion, in the Book of Revelation, we have also seen a revelation of believers transformed into the "image of His Son." Revelation is also an amazing revelation of the church, God's body, created in His image, as was originally intended in Genesis 1:26,27.

The final message given to John confirms the comments at the beginning of our study: "Do not seal the words of the prophecy of this book, for the time is at hand!" (Revelation 22:10) The time has come for the "Unsealing of the Book" and we have seen together the revelation of Jesus Christ to and in His Church!

These words are indeed open for our understanding and not complex to comprehend.

APPENDICES

APPENDICES

CHARTS

APPENDIX I

Chart of Book of Revelation

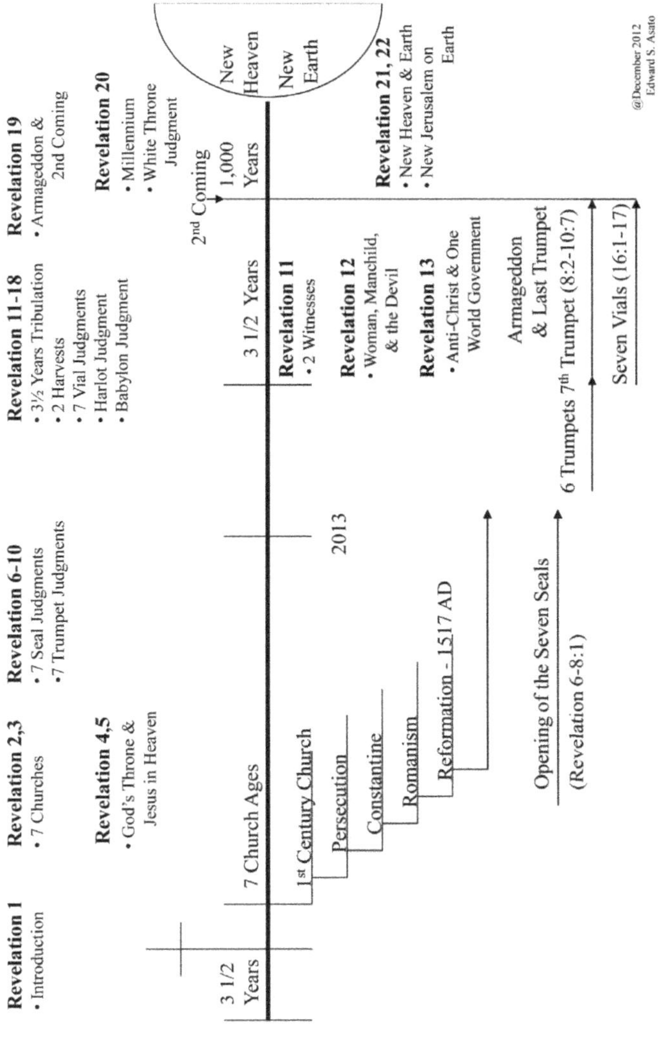

APPENDIX II
The Old Testament & Revelation

Summary: The Old Testament and New Testament Scriptures are one unified revelation of God's purposes for man on earth.

Jesus & the Apostle's Bible

In the 1st century, Jesus, His disciples and Paul had one Bible from which they preached the gospel. They only had the Old Testament Scriptures. It was later in the century that New Testament books were written. It was not until the mid-300 AD that the New Testament scriptures were officially canonized.

The Old Testament in the New Testament

The New Testament could never be written without the Old Testament scriptures. Like separate streams flowing down a mountain into a vast ocean below, many Old Testament books flowed into the vast ocean of New Testament revelation. To fully understand New Testament insights, a student needs a healthy grasp of the streams of Old Testament passages, characters, events and stories.

"The New Testament is in the Old Testament concealed. The Old Testament is in the New Testament revealed." "The New is in the Old enfolded. The Old is in the New unfolded." "The New is in the Old contained. The Old is in the New explained."

The New cannot exist without the Old. The Bible is one book. Both are needed for a complete revelation of God's plan for man and the earth.

The Old & New Testaments Compared

In the book of Matthew alone, there are 40 quotations and over 100 allusions taken from the Old Testament. In the Book of Revelation, there are over 400.

To fully understand the Book of Revelation, students need to interconnect Old Testament quotations and allusions. Clarity, insight and illumination would be the result. Employing the use of commentaries suggested in the Bibliography would be helpful in pursuing the study of Revelation.

Irving L. Jensen points out that Revelation's 404 verses contain 550 Old Testament references. Merrill C. Tenny in "Interpreting Revelation" estimated it contains 348 quotations or allusions. This chart is a breakdown of Tenny's study of those Old Testament books.

DISTRIBUTION OF OLD TESTAMENT QUOTATIONS & ALLUSIONS IN THE BOOK OF REVELATION

DISTRIBUTION BY SECTIONS		
Section	**Reference**	**Number**
Prologue	1:1-8	11
Vision I	1:9-3:22	38
Vision II	4:1-16:21	164
Vision III	17:1-21:8	95
Vision IV	21:9-22:5	24
Vision V	22:6-21	16
		Total 348

DISTRIBUTION BY BOOKS OF THE OLD TESTAMENT

Books	Number	Books	Number
Genises	13	Psalms	43
Exodus	27	Proverbs	2
Leviticus	4	**Poetry**	**45**
Numbers	3	Isaiah	79
Deuteronomy	10	Jeremiah	22
Pentateuch	**57**	Ezekiel	43
Joshua	1	Daniel	53
Judges	1	**Major Prophets**	**197**
II Samuel	1	Hosea	2
II Kings	6	Joel	8
I Chronicles	1	Amos	9
Nehemiah	1	Habakkuk	1
Historical	**11**	Zephaniah	2
		Zechariah	15
		Malachi	1
		Minor Prophets	**38**

[1] "Interpreting Revelation", Merrill C. Tenny, Grand Rapids, Michigan, Wm B. Eerdmans Publishing Company, 1957.

APPENDIX III
Matthew 24 and Revelation

Summary: What John saw and wrote in Revelation parallels what Jesus predicted in His prophetic teachings in Matthew 24.

Revelation & Matthew 24 Parallels

1. Jesus predicted the emergence of false Christ and prophets in unfolding last day events. Matthew 24:4,5,11,23,26 John saw similar events in Revelation 13:1-9 and 13:10-18.
2. Jesus prophesied an increase of wars among nations in the final days. Matthew 24:6,7 John also saw global warfare taking place at the time of the end. Revelation 6:3,4.
3. Famines were included in Jesus' prediction of things to come. Matthew 24:7 John paralleled what Jesus prophesied. Revelation 6:5,6
4. Jesus predicted the rise of pandemics as a major concern in the world today. Matthew 24:7 John predicted the same. Revelation 6:7,8
5. Jesus saw a global increase of the frequency and intensity of earthquakes. Matthew 24:7 John was also given visions of terrifying earthquakes shaking the world. Revelation 6:12
6. Jesus envisioned the chaotic patterns of the sun, moon and stars. Matthew 24:29 John saw similar events taking place. Revelation 6:13-17
7. Persecution of Christians globally is on the rise today exactly as Jesus predicted. Matthew 24:9,10,21,22. When the 5^{thth} seal was opened, John saw martyrs for Christ around the throne of God. Revelation 6:9-11; 7:14
8. Today, two of seven people on earth are believers. The church is experiencing a time of worldwide harvest such as Jesus taught. Matthew 24:14 John was also shown this harvest. Revelation 14:14-16
9. Jesus prophesied that Israel would be restored as a nation after 2,000 years of wandering. Matthew 24:32 John also saw

Israel recognized as a nation and swept into Jesus' spiritual family, His church. Revelation 1:7; 7:4; 11:1,2,8; 14:1

10. And, finally, Jesus clearly explained His second coming as a global and visible event. Matthew 24:27,28,30,31 John also confirmed this visible and global event. Revelation 1:7; 19:11-15

APPENDIX IV
The Tabernacle of Moses

Summary: The Tabernacle of Moses' furniture, ceremonies and blueprint contains prophetic pictures of Jesus, church history, the restoration of Biblical truth and a template for the Book of Revelation.

The 1st century church not only taught doctrine from passages and references of the OT, it also utilized OT personalities, events, religious ceremonies and buildings to explain prophecies of things to come.

The book of Hebrews introduces us to the Tabernacle of Moses and how it contained prophetic pictures of the redemptive ministry of Jesus Christ. And, in further study of the Tabernacle, we will discover that Moses' Tabernacle also contained prophetic insights into the Church Age.

Hebrews & Moses' Tabernacle

The book of Hebrews reveals that the sacrifices, priesthood and furniture of the Tabernacle of Moses are prophetic types of Jesus Christ and future events.

Throughout Hebrews 8-11, Moses' Tabernacle is presented as a pattern of a greater heavenly reality. (Hebrews 8:5; 9:9,11; 10:1,11-14) The covenant, priesthood, ceremonies, furniture and sacrifices are images of who Jesus is and what He did.

Speaking of the furniture, Hebrews 9:1-5 says, "Of these things we cannot now speak in detail." (v.5) Clearly, there were more numerous prophetic connections the author wanted to explain. Over the church's two millennium, Bible teachers have understood some of the things the Hebrew writer had in mind.

In this short overview, we will see God's prophetic blueprint embedded in the Tabernacle of Moses in four areas: 1) Jesus Christ, 2) Bible History, 3) The restoration of Biblical truths, and 4) The template of the Tabernacle in the book of Revelation.

I. Jesus in the Tabernacle

Jesus has traditionally been revealed through the pieces of furniture in the Tabernacle of Moses. Notice the following:

Jesus is seen in the Brazen Altar used to sacrifice and shed the blood of lambs. Jesus is our Lamb, who took away our sins. (Exodus 12:1-14 & John 1:29)

The Brazen Laver was where the priests washed themselves after offering bloody animal sacrifices. This furniture pictures Jesus in the act of baptism at the hands of John the Baptist and pictures the pure and holy life He lived. (Exodus 30:17-21 & Mathew 3:13)

Jesus is seen in the Table of Showbread. He multiplied bread and taught that He was the Bread of Life. (Exodus 25:23-30 & John 6:10-13)

Jesus declared He was the Light of the World as a fulfillment of the 7-branched Candlestick. (Exodus 25:31-40 & John 9:1-7) Jesus Christ is also displayed as our Intercessor in the candlesticks. (Exodus 30:1ff & John 17:1-26, Hebrews 5:7; 7:25)

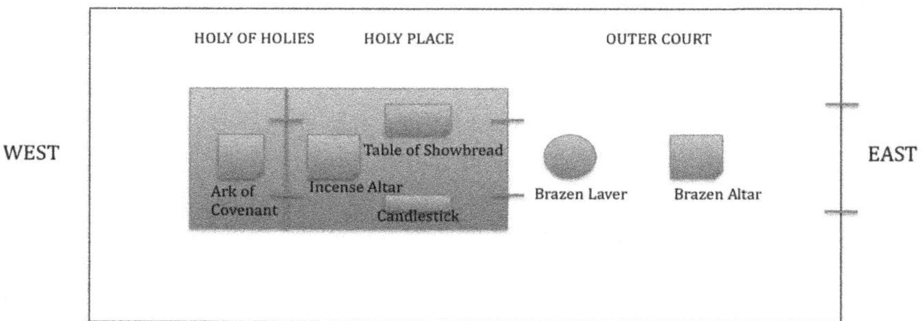

The High Priest sprinkled the lamb's blood on the Mercy Seat. Jesus is our High Priest who covered the Mercy Seat ("propitiation", Greek) with His own blood. (Exodus 25:10-22 & Romans 3:25; I John 2:2)

II. Bible and Church History In Moses' Tabernacle

In the dimensions of the tabernacle, we uncover God's prophetic timetable related to the 7 days of creation. This prophetic measurement of time is described in II Peter 3:8 as "unto the Lord a day is as 1,000 years." Applying it to the days of creation, history could be divided into a 7,000-year period.

The first 2,000 years marks the time from Adam to Abraham. The next 500 years covers Abraham's life to the time of Moses. From Moses till the coming of Jesus is a period of 1,500 years. The period of the Church Age amounts to about 2,000 years of history. And, finally, the Book of Revelation predicts a coming 1,000-year millennium rule of Jesus Christ upon the earth.

Amazingly, embedded in the dimensions of the Tabernacle, we discover the three periods of the Law (1,500), the Church (2,000) and the Millennium reign (1,000) of Jesus Christ.

The dimension of the fence around the tabernacle is 1,500 cubits. ([100 +100 + 50 +50] x 5 = 1,500, Exodus 27:18) The dimension of the Holy Place is 2,000 cubits. (20x10x10 = 2,000, Exodus 36:21,23,27,28) And the dimension of the Holy of Holies is 1,000 cubits.(10x10x10 = 1,000, Exodus 36:21,23,27,28) These describes the period of Law, the Church and the Millennium.

III. The Restoration of Truth in the Tabernacle

We also see the restoration of Bible truth in the history of the church. As each truth was restored, denominations sprung up.

The Brazen Altar was where the lamb's blood was shed and represented the Protestant Reformation led by Martin Luther in 1517 and begun the Lutheran denomination.

The Brazen Laver was where the priests cleansed themselves and represented the subsequent Baptist and Holiness movement in the early 1600-1700s that created the Baptist and Holiness denominations.

The Table of Showbread provided bread for the priests and prefigured Bible teaching churches across America in the 1800s.

The Golden Candlestick gave light by burning oil and represented the Pentecostal revival begun in the early 1900s that has given the gospel to nations globally.

The Altar of Incense signifies the global movements of prayer and worship begun over the past few decades.

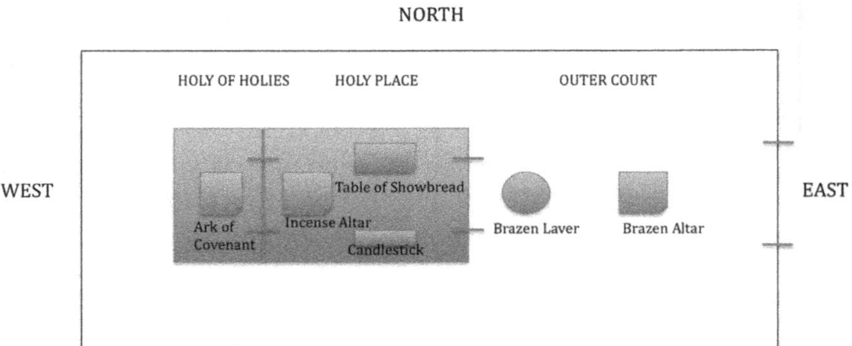

The Ark of the Covenant in the Holy of Holies seem to point to the final stages of revival on the earth where the "glory of God will fill the earth." All past historic movements seem to point to this time fulfilling the church's prayer of God's kingdom coming on earth.

IV. Revelation and Moses' Tabernacle

Images of Moses' Tabernacle appear repeatedly in this book to demonstrate how God uses it as a template for prophecies.

Tabernacle Imagery in Revelation

In chapter one, we are introduced to the Holy Place with seven candlesticks (1:12,13,20) and Jesus as High Priest officiating in it. (1:13-15)

In chapters two and three, Jesus' comments and promised rewards are steeped with Tabernacle images – seven golden candlesticks (2:1,5), tree of life (with implied two guarding cherubim) (2:7), crown (bordering the furnitures) (2:10), manna and white stone (2:17), rod of iron (as Aaron's rod) (2:27), priest's garments (3:5,18) pillar of the temple (3:12) and the throne (mercy seat and His voice heard) (3:20,21)

The sea of glass before God's throne in chapter four is reminiscent of the brazen laver. (4:6; 15:2) The clothing of the twenty-four elders, their garments and crowns positioned around the throne of God are images of the ark and priests. (4:4)

The slain Lamb further infers the brazen altar used for animal sacrifices in chapter five. (5:6) Throughout Revelation, Jesus as the Lamb is referenced 27 times and dominates His unique description as He issues these final days of judgment.

These beginning five chapters introduce us to the imagery of the Tabernacle of Moses used in the Book of Revelation. Revelation uses the Tabernacle as a template for understanding God's conclusion to divine history for the last days.

God is Sovereign over Last Day Judgments

The temple and throne of God are mentioned repeatedly in this book. The word "throne" occurs over 39 times and "temple" used 16 times. The "temple" and "throne" are the heavenly substance for the Ark of the Covenant and the Holy of Holies.

The following are some of the thirty-nine verses mentioning the "throne": 1:4; 3:21; 4:2-6,9,10; 5:1,6,7,11,13; 6:16; 7:9-11,15,17; 8:3; 12:5; 14:3,5 and 16:7.

The following are some of the sixteen verses mentioning the "temple": 3:12; 7:15; 11:1,2,19; 14:15,17; 15:5,8 and 16:1.

The Major Lesson from these occurrences of "temple" and "throne" demonstrate conclusively that *God is Sovereign and in total control* of the events of the last day judgment upon the earth.

The release of three sets of seven judgments demonstrates how the Tabernacle is used as a template to understand God's last day judgments. Earth's judgments demonstrate a movement from the Outer Court flowing into the Holy of Holies.

I. *The Outer Court and the Brazen Altar:* The Slain Lamb of God releases the Seven Seal judgments. This assumes an activity occurring at the Brazen Altar in the Outer Court of the Tabernacle. In chapter six, John sees each seal opened by the Lamb of God, Jesus Christ. (6:1,3,5,7,9,12; 8:1)

II. *The Holy Place and the Altar of Incense:* Seven angels positioned by the Incense Altar in the Holy Place blow the Seven Trumpets of judgments. (8:2-6,7,8,12; 9:1,13; 10:7; 11:15,19) This brings us one step further into the inner chamber of God.

III. *The Holy of Holies and the Temple of God:* The final seven vial judgments are issued from the temple of God through another seven angels and prepare the earth for the coming kingdom of God. (15:1,5-8; 16:1-4,8,10,12,17) This ushers us into the Holiest of All, the place of God's glory in the Tabernacle.

A Further Lesson reveals God's ultimate purpose of establishing His kingdom on earth as the abiding place for His church. The final day judgment is cleansing the earth to prepare for that ultimate destiny.

Chapter twenty-one finally describes heavenly Jerusalem descending upon the earth and the throne and temple of God being established in this world. (21:1-6) The earth becomes the Holy of Holies where God's presence dwells with His people. (21:16) Precious stones from the breastplate of the High Priest are seen comprising the foundation of that City. (20:19,20)

God's plan has prepared the earth and His church to fulfill His highest purpose. He has used the entrance into the Holy of Holies as the image to convey that ultimate destiny. The prayer "Your kingdom come, Your will be done on earth as it is in heaven" will be finally fulfilled.

APPENDIX V
The Feasts of Israel

Summary: The Seven Feasts of Israel contain past, present and future prophetic images of Jesus, Israel and the church.

Introduction

God established the Seven Feasts of Israel as an annual celebration of remembrance and religious ceremonies. Amazingly, it also contained prophetic pictures of God's purposes for the Messiah, Israel, and His church.

The Seven Feasts were held on the 1st, 3rd and 7th months annually. The first three feasts are grouped together and called the Passover Feast. The fourth stands alone by its name, Pentecost. And the last three feasts are grouped together and called the Tabernacle Feast.

I. The Passover Feast: Jesus fulfilled this feast through His death, burial and resurrection.

The Passover Feast (Leviticus 23:5) was fulfilled in Jesus Christ. He was the Passover Lamb. (I Corinthians 5:7) On the same night that Israel was preparing their lambs for their annual Passover Feast, Jesus was being arrested and sentenced for crucifixion.

The Unleavened Bread Feast (Leviticus 23:5) was fulfilled in Jesus' sinless life crucified for us. (2 Corinthians 5:21) Leaven was used as a picture of sin in the Bible. Jesus' sinless body lay in the tomb during the first days of this feast.

The First Fruits Feast (Leviticus 23:10) pointed to Jesus' resurrection as the first fruits of the righteous. He resurrected on this very feast day, so Paul refers to Jesus as the "first fruits from the dead." (I Corinthians 15:20)

II. The Feast of Pentecost: The church fulfilled this feast in the first century on the day of Pentecost.

This Feast of Pentecost (Leviticus 23:16) occurred fifty days after the Passover Feast and was fulfilled at the outpouring of the Holy Spirit, the birth of the church and initial harvest of Jewish and Gentiles souls in the Book of Acts. (Acts 2:1-4; 41)

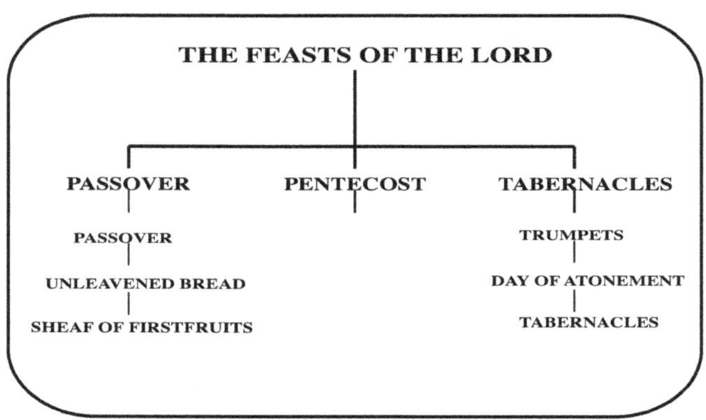

The Past & Future Fulfillment of the Feasts

God fulfilled the Passover and Pentecost feasts through Jesus' death, resurrection and the outpouring of the Spirit upon His church. Because the first four feasts were fulfilled in the past history of the church, their fulfillment provides the basis for the expectation of the fulfillment of the Feast of Trumpets, Day of Atonement and the Tabernacle feasts sometime today and further in the future of the church.

When we investigate each of these feasts separately, we will discover that God is indeed at work today in the fulfillment of these feasts currently.

The following explanation suggests some possible future scenarios of their fulfillment.

III. The Feast of Tabernacles: The church is seeing the beginning fulfillment of these feasts today.

The Feast of Trumpets (Leviticus 23:24) can be understood by the purpose trumpets were used in Israel. Trumpets gathered and united Israel's leaders, signaled Israel's move to their next wilderness destination, called their assembly, announced their feast days and blasted a preparation for war. (Numbers 10:1-10)

God is today gathering and uniting the church beyond denominational differences. He is also signaling prophets to guide the church toward their next destination and movement. Today, conferences for leaders and believers are being conducted globally. And both Israel and the church are preparing for battle.

While God is fulfilling trumpets in Israel and His church, it is also interesting to note that one of the series of judgments mentioned in Revelation is called the *Seven Trumpet Judgments.*

The Day of Atonement (Leviticus 23:27) was when the High Priest entered the Holy of Holies once a year to officiate in covering the sins of Israel for another year. God is doing the same thing today in dealing with holiness and righteousness in His Church. The message of grace and righteousness are revealing what God has done on the cross to cover all our sins.

Also, the Book of Revelation uses Day of Atonement language of entering the temple, viewing the Ark and describing the High priest's garments and ministry. (11:19; 15:5-8)

The Feast of Tabernacles (Leviticus 23:34) was a great time of harvest and called the Feast of Booths, where celebration for the harvest was accompanied by living in tents away from home. This seems to point to the final end time harvest, the 2nd coming of Jesus Christ, the receiving of Jesus by the nation of Israel and the kingdom of God coming to the earth. All these events are clearly described in the Book of Revelation.

APPENDIX VI
Bible Numeric

Summary: Numbers possess hidden images and meanings of spiritual truth. They have great significance in the Bible.

The Number Seven

For example, the number *7* expresses completion and perfection. There were *7* days of creation, *7* years of Egypt's harvest and famine, *7* Feasts of Israel, a *7*-day march around Jericho and many other sevens pointing to completion and perfection.

The Book of Revelation begins with *7* candlesticks representing the *7* churches. (Revelation 1:20) This is one of the 54 times the number *7* is used in the Book of Revelation. This seems to indicate that the prophecies in this book point to the completion of God's purposes for His church on the earth.

The Number Twelve

The number 12 is also symbolic. It is a number for divine government. God gave Israel 12 sons for their 12 tribes. When Jesus began His apostolic team, He chose 12 men.

As we get a glimpse of heaven and God's throne, we see the number 12 used solely to represent heaven's leaders. (Revelation 4:4,10) Around the throne are 24 elders or a multiple of 12 (12 x 2). This picture seems to indicate a government structure in heaven that was foreshadowed on earth in Israel and with the apostles. This indicates that God is governing and totally in charge of what unfolds throughout the book of Revelation.

The Number One Hundred Forty-Four Thousand

The use of the number 144,000 is also a multiple of 12 (12,000 x 12). Most interestingly, when David was king over Israel, he set up a government filled with multiples of 12.

David chose 24,000 priests (2,000 x 12) to look after the house of God. (I Chronicles 23:3) He chose 24 leaders to oversee groups of 1,000 priests. (24:7-19) The musicians for worship were also arranged in groups of 24. (2 x 12) (25:7-31) His military division of leaders was organized into 12 groups of 24,000 each. (27:1-15) The number 12 fills the structure of David's government as recorded in I Chronicles.

The appearance of 12 is so frequently used in the book of Revelation that it confirms that God's government is totally in control of the events of the end times. This also reveals that God is grooming leaders to fulfill His final purposes for His church and His people Israel.

APPENDIX VII
The 10 Plagues of Egypt & Revelation

***Summary*:** God uses the imagery of the 10 plagues of Egypt to demonstrate that His judgment targets the world, not His people. He will provide for and protect His people amidst the judgment.

God's Purposes:

What was God's purpose for the 10 plagues?

1) It confirmed Abraham's Covenant. (See Appendix XII),
2) It freed Israel from Egyptian slavery,
3) It revealed God's glory to Israel & Egypt,
4) It showed God's favor in protecting Israel and judging Egypt,
5) It annihilated Egypt's power,
6) It released Israel to their destiny to inherit Canaan,
7) It positioned Israel to rule nations through Solomon.

The Lesson: What God did physically and materially for Israel, He will do spiritually for His church in the time of the end.

The 1st Plague & 2nd Trumpet, 2 Witnesses, 2nd & 3rd Vials

Exodus 7:20 – The 1st Plague of Blood: "And Moses ... lifted up the rod and struck the *waters* ... And all the *waters* in the river were turned to *blood*. (7:20)

Revelation 8:8 - The 2nd Trumpet: "Then the second angel sounded: And something like a great mountain burning with fire was thrown into the *sea*, and a third of the *sea* became *blood*" (8:8)

Revelation 11:6 – Two Witnesses: "These have power ... over *waters* to turn them to *blood*, and to strike the earth with all plagues, as often as they desire."

Revelation 16:3,4 – 2nd & 3rd Vials: "Then the second angel poured out his bowl on the *sea*, and it became *blood* as of a dead man ...Then the third angel poured out his bowl on the *rivers* and *springs* of *water*, and they became *blood*."

The 2nd Plague & the 6th Vial

Exodus 8:6 - The 2nd Plague of Frogs: "So Aaron stretched out his hand over the waters of Egypt, and the *frogs* came up and covered the land of Egypt."

Revelation 16:12,13 - The 6th Vial: "Then the sixth angel poured out his bowl ... so that ... the kings from the east might be prepared. And I saw three unclean spirits like *frogs* coming out ... of the dragon, ... the beast, ...the false prophet."

The 3rd Plague of Lice - None

Exodus 8:17 - The 3rd Plague of Lice: "... Aaron stretched out his hand with his rod and struck the dust of the earth, and it became *lice* on man and beast. All the dust of the land became *lice* throughout all the land of Egypt."

Revelation - None

The 4th Plague of Flies & the 4th Seal

Exodus 8:21 - The 4th Plague of Flies: "...I will send swarms [of *flies*] on you ... your servants, ...your people and into your houses. The houses ... shall be full of swarms [of *flies*]...." (Flies could also be translated "wild *beasts*" in Hebrew.)

Revelation 6:7,8 - The 4th Seal: "...He opened the fourth seal ... and behold, a pale horse ... who sat on it was Death, and Hades .... And power was given ... over a fourth of the earth, to kill ... by the *beasts* of the earth."

The 5th Plague of Pestilences & the 4th Seal

Exodus 9:3 - The 5th Plague of Pestilences: ""behold, the hand of the LORD will be on your cattle in the field, on the horses, on the donkeys, on the camels, on the oxen, and on the sheep--a very severe *pestilence*."

Revelation 6:7,8 - The 4th Seal: "...He opened the fourth seal ... and behold, a pale horse ... who sat on it was Death, and Hades .... And power was given ... over a fourth of the earth, to kill ... with *death*." (Death can be translated "*Pestilences*" in Greek.)

The 6th Plague & the 1st Vial Judgment

Exodus 9:10 - The 6th Plague of Boils: "Then they took ashes from the furnace ... and Moses scattered [them] toward heaven. And [they] caused *boils* that break out in *sores* on man and beast."

Revelation 16:2 - The 1st Vial: "And the first went, and poured out his bowl (*vial*) ... and a foul... loathsome *sore* upon the men which had the mark of the beast..."

The 7th Plague & the 1st Trumpet & 7th Vial

Exodus 9:23 - The 7th Plague of Hail: "And Moses stretched out his rod ... and the LORD sent thunder and *hail* ... the LORD rained *hail* on the land of Egypt."

Revelation 8:7 - The 1st Trumpet: "The first angel sounded: and *hail* and fire followed mingled with blood, and they were thrown to the earth...."

Revelation 16:21 – The 7tht Vial: "And there fell upon men a great *hail* out of heaven, [every stone] about the weight of a talent..." (a talent is about 60-90 pounds)

The 8th Plague of Locusts & the 5th Trumpet

Exodus 10:13 - The 8th Plague of Locusts: "So Moses stretched out his rod ...and the LORD brought an east wind ... When it was morning, the east wind brought the *locusts*."

Revelation 9:3,4 - The 1st Trumpet: "Then out of the smoke *locusts* came upon the earth... And to them was given power, as the scorpions of the earth have power."

The 9th Plague & the 5th Vial

Exodus 10:21 - The 9th Plague of Darkness: "And the LORD said to Moses, Stretch out your hand toward heaven, that there may be *darkness* over the land ... darkness [which] may even be felt."

Revelation 9:3,4 - The 5th Vial: "And the fifth angel poured out his vial upon the seat of the beast; and his kingdom was full of *darkness*; and they gnawed their tongues for pain."

The 10th Plague Death & the 4th Seal, 6th Trumpet, Final War

Exodus 11:4,5 - The 10th Plague of Darkness: "And Moses said, Thus says the LORD ... all the firstborn in the land of Egypt shall *die*, from the firstborn of Pharaoh ... even to the firstborn of the female servant ... the firstborn of the animals."

Revelation 6:8 - The 4th Seal: "... behold a pale horse: and the name of him that sat on it was *Death* ... power was given ... over the fourth of the earth, to kill with sword ... hunger ... *death*, and by the beasts of the earth."

Revelation 9:14,15 - The 6th Trumpet: "Saying to the sixth angel which had the trumpet, 'Loose the four angels...' And the four angels were loosed, ... for to *slay the third part of men*."

Revelation 19:21 - 2nd Coming: "And the remnant were *slain* with the sword of Him that sat upon the horse..."

APPENDIX VIII
The 70-Week Prophecy of Daniel

***Summary*:** Daniel's 70-Week Prophecy covers 490 years. The first 483 years climax with Jesus' baptism in water. The final 7 years contains - the 1st 3.5 year period of Jesus' ministry and crucifixion and the 2nd 3.5 years leads to Jesus' 2nd Coming.

The Background & Context

Judah was taken into Babylonian captivity, but their release was imminent.

Based on Jeremiah's prophecy (Jeremiah 29:10), the end of this captivity period had come and Daniel began interceding for the fulfillment of that prophecy. During this time of fasting and prayer, the angel Gabriel was sent to Daniel and revealed the 70-Week Prophecy.

Interpreting the Prophecy: Daniel 9:2,24-17

The General Time Period: This prophecy establishes a period of time in human history referred to as "Seventy weeks" that amounts to 490 days (70x7). (v.24a)

But "days", interpreted prophetically, is "a year for a day" (Numbers 14:34 & Ezekiel 4:6) and represents a period of 490 "years" carved out of human history to fulfill God's purposes "for your people (Israel) and for your holy city." (Jerusalem)(v.24b)

God's Past & Future Purpose: And God clearly states His intention for this period - "to finish transgression, to put an end to sin, to atone for wickedness, to bring in everlasting righteousness, to seal up the vision and prophecy and to anoint the most holy." (v.24c)

Clearly, this prophecy has a past and future fulfillment.

In the past, Jesus Christ came to cleanse man's sins through His death on the cross. He came "to finish transgression ... to atone for wickedness..."

In the future, the elements yet to be fulfilled are: "... to put an end to sin ... to bring in everlasting righteousness, to seal up the vision and prophecy and to anoint the most holy." These have not yet happened. They represent the climactic fulfillment of the crucifixion of Jesus Christ.

When the Messiah Would Come. The starting point of this prophecy is clear - "...the decree to restore and rebuild Jerusalem..." (v.25a) Judah would return from Babylonian captivity and begin to restore their ruined city, Jerusalem.

From historical documents, we can accurately conclude that date as 457 BC. That is our starting point. So, we begin at 457 BC.

Included in this starting point is a parenthetical period of 49 years or "Seven weeks" (v.25b) during which time the walls of the city were rebuilt. This took place with much opposition - "it will be rebuilt ... in times of trouble"(v.25c) as explained in both the books of Ezra and Nehemiah. This brings us to 434 BC.

The next time period involves the introduction of the "Messiah, the Prince" to the world. That "Messiah" was Jesus Christ. Jesus did not begin His Messianic ministry at His birth but at His water baptism. He became the "Messiah" ("Anointed One") when the Holy Spirit descended upon (anointed) Him as a dove. (Matthew 3:16,17) It was at that time that Jesus Christ was introduced as the "Messiah" to His people.

That brings us to 26 AD, when Jesus was baptized and began His ministry.

The Messiah's Ministry

Jesus was the "seed" of Abraham (Galatians 3:16) and came to fulfill the Abrahamic Covenant. (See Appendix XII) "He will confirm the covenant with many for "one week." (v.27a) The 1st half or 1st 3.5 years was a time of blessings announced by Jesus as the "acceptable year of the Lord." (Luke 4:19) and the last 3.5 years was described as a time of "the day of the vengeance of our God." (Isaiah 61:2b)

"In the middle of the seven week", or after the 1st 3.5 years, Jesus will "put an end to sacrifice and offering." (v.27b) Every Old Testament sacrifice pointed to the ultimate sacrifice of Jesus Christ as God's Lamb. His crucifixion brought "an end to sacrifice and offering", once and for all. (Hebrew 9:12,25,26)

Daniel also saw that "the Messiah will be cut off but not for Himself." (v.26a) Jesus wouldn't die for Himself, but for the sins of the world. In the NIV, it says, "the Anointed One will be cut off and will have nothing." (v.26a; John 19:23,24) Jesus died for others and was left with nothing. The Roman soldiers that crucified Him also took His clothing. He was left with nothing. But history records that three days later He rose from the dead.

So, the 1st 3.5 years ended with Jesus' death, burial and resurrection.

But there's a missing 3.5 years in the 70-Week Prophecy.

The Missing 3.5 Years

Where is the missing 3.5 years of Daniel's prophecy?

While the church is looking for a 7 year Tribulation, the Book of Revelation refers only to a 3.5 year time period. Nothing is said about 7 years. In Revelation 11-13, we discover that a 3.5 years period is mentioned four times. (11:2,3; 12:6,14; 13:5) Clearly, this is the period of the "day of the vengeance of our God," the 2nd or last 3.5 years. (Isaiah 61:2)

In His first coming, Jesus came to fulfill the "blessing" of the Abrahamic Covenant. "I will bless those that bless you." (Genesis 12:3; Galatians 3:13,14)

In His second coming, Jesus will fulfill the "judgment" aspect of the Abrahamic Covenant - "I will curse them that curse you." (Genesis 12:3) The ungodly world will persecute the church and Jesus Christ and will warrant the unsealing of the series of judgments revealed in the Book of Revelation.

The 70-Week Prophecy also predicted the destruction of Jerusalem and the temple - "The people of the prince ... will destroy the city and the sanctuary." (v.26b) And in 70 AD, Titus, the Roman General, led his troops to fulfill that prophetic word.

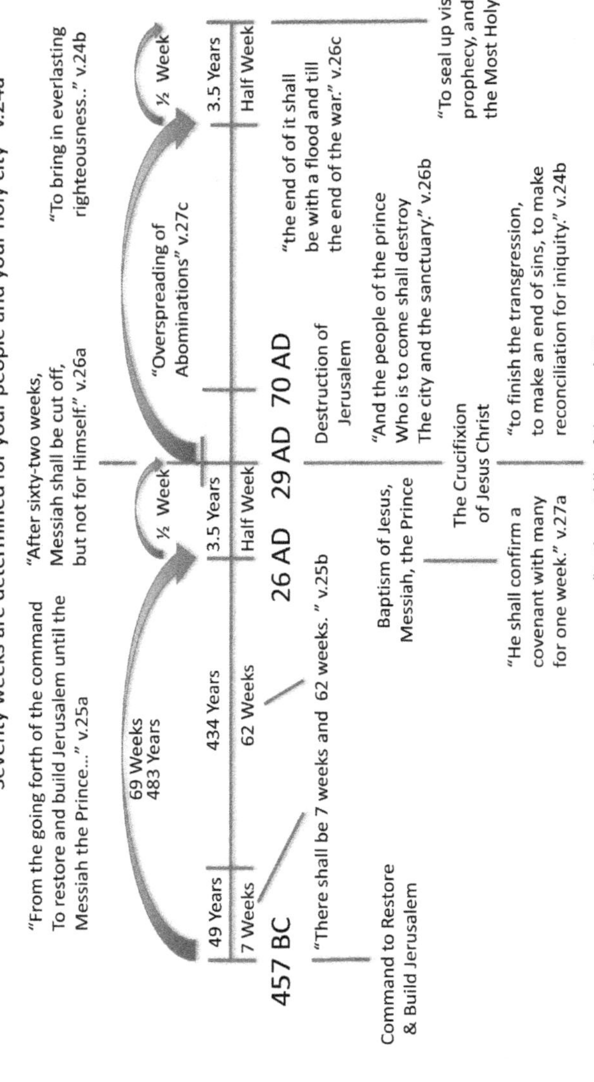
DANIEL'S 70 WEEK PROPHECY
Daniel 9:24-27
"Seventy weeks are determined for your people and your holy city" v.24a
"From the going forth of the command To restore and build Jerusalem until the Messiah the Prince..." v.25a
"After sixty-two weeks, Messiah shall be cut off, but not for Himself." v.26a
"To bring in everlasting righteousness.." v.24b
69 Weeks
483 Years
½ Week
"Overspreading of Abominations" v.27c
½ Week
49 Years
434 Years
3.5 Years
3.5 Years
7 Weeks
62 Weeks
Half Week
Half Week
457 BC
26 AD
29 AD
70 AD
"There shall be 7 weeks and 62 weeks. " v.25b
Destruction of Jerusalem
"the end of of it shall be with a flood and till the end of the war." v.26c
"And the people of the prince Who is to come shall destroy The city and the sanctuary." v.26b
"To seal up vision and prophecy, and anoint the Most Holy." v.24b
Command to Restore & Build Jerusalem
Baptism of Jesus, Messiah, the Prince
The Crucifixion of Jesus Christ
"to finish the transgression, to make an end of sins, to make reconciliation for iniquity." v.24b
"He shall confirm a covenant with many for one week." v.27a
"In the middle of the week, He shall bring and end to sacrifice and offering." 27b

They devastated Jerusalem and the Jewish sanctuary. Since that time, Israel has been scattered across the nations of the world, not to return until May 14, 1948.

The Gap of 2,000 Years

Why is nothing said about the gap of 2,000 years of history between the 1st half and the 2nd half of the 7 years in Daniel's 70-Week Prophecy?

Something is said, but only briefly.

It describe the climate of the world, the result of the Jewish nation's rejection of their Messiah and the final climax of world history.

The prophecy tells us that the world will be filled with conflicts and global warfare. "War will continue until the end..." (v.26c) This agrees with Jesus' prediction in Matthew 24:6,7 and John's Revelation 6:4.

As a result of the Jewish rejection of their Messiah, their temple sacrifices were to be offered in vain. Because the "Lamb of God that takes away the sins of the world" (John 1:29) has come, the Jew's rejection of Jesus' sacrifice is "an abomination that causes desolation" (v.27b) and, as a result, "desolations have been decreed" (v.26c). Everything the Jews now do in rendering sacrifices and offerings are vain and empty motions. ("Desolate")

And, finally, world history will be climaxed with a flood of ungodliness and God's judgment. "The end will come like a flood." (v.26c). As the flood of Noah took away the ungodly to God's judgment, so will the flood of deception take away the ungodly at the 2nd Coming of Jesus Christ. (Luke 17:26)

In the Book of Revelation, we are presented with the 3 series of 7 Seals, Trumpets and Vial Judgments upon the world. Through those judgments, we uncover the final climax of God's purpose for mankind - "the consummation which is determined." (v.27c)

APPENDIX IX
Daniel & Revelation

***Summary*:** The books of Daniel and John's Revelation were written 600 years apart from each other, yet the similarities are amazing. Their visions validate the Sovereign God of all history inspiring both prophetic insights.

The 2nd Coming of Christ

Daniel 7:13,14 - "I saw in the night visions, and behold, one like the Son of man came with the clouds of heaven... all ... nations ... should serve him: his dominion is an everlasting dominion and his kingdom that which shall not be destroyed."

Revelation 19:11 - "And I saw heaven opened, and behold a white horse; and he that sat upon him [was] called Faithful and True, and in righteousness he doth judge and make war."

The 10 Kings of the Time of the End

Daniel 7:24 - "And the ten horns out of this kingdom are ten kings that shall arise; and another shall rise after them; and he shall be diverse from the first, and he shall subdue three kings."

Revelation 13:1 - "And I stood upon the sand of the sea, and saw a beast rise up out of the sea, having seven heads and ten horns, and upon his horns ten crowns and upon his heads the name of blasphemy."

The Resurrection of the Dead

Daniel 12:2 - "And many of them that sleep in the dust of the earth shall awake, some to everlasting life, some to shame and everlasting contempt."

Revelation 20:11 - "And I saw the dead, small and great, standing before God, and books were opened. And another book was opened, which is the Book of Life. And the dead were judged out of those things which were written in the books, according to their works."

Three and a Half Years

Daniel 7:25 - "And he shall speak great words against the most High, and shall wear out the saints of the most High, and think to change times and laws: and they shall be given into his hands until a time and times and the dividing of time. "

Revelation 12:14 - "And to the woman were given two wings of a great eagle that she might fly into the wilderness, into her place, where she is nourished for a time and times and half a time, from the face of the serpent."

The Great Tribulation

Daniel 12:1 - "And at that time shall Michael stand up ... there shall be a time of trouble, such as never was since there was a nation even to that same time: and at that time thy people shall be delivered ... "

Revelation 7:14 – "And I said to him, "Sir, you know." So he said to me, 'These are the ones who come out of great tribulation, and washed their robes and made them white in the blood of the Lamb."

The Anti-Christ

Daniel 7:7 - " After this I saw in the night visions, and behold a fourth beast, dreadful and terrible and strong exceedingly; ...it devoured and brake in pieces, and stamped the residue with the feet of it: and it was diverse from all the beasts that were before it; and it had ten horns."

Revelation 13:1 - "And I stood upon the sand of the sea, and saw a beast rise up out of the sea, having seven heads and ten horns, and upon his horns ten crowns, and upon his heads the name of blasphemy."

The Archangel Michael

Daniel 12:1 - "...Michael stand up, the great prince which stands for the children of your people: and there shall be a time of trouble...."

Revelation 12:7 - "And there was war in heaven: Michael and his angels fought against the dragon; and the dragon fought and his angels."

APPENDIX X
The War of Armageddon

Summary: Ezekiel 38 & 39 and Revelation 19 predict the War of Armageddon and earth's final days.[1] [Note: This lesson presents an alternative perspective including the possibility that the USA and Europe might be involved along with Israel.]

Ezekiel 38-39 is the most divinely affirmed prophecy in the entire Bible! The phrase "Thus says the Lord God" occurs seven times in these chapters. (38:3,10,14,17 and 39:1,17,25) No other prophecy in the Bible is so divinely stamped with those words of declaration. This "Sevenfold Affirmation" indicates that this prophecy will be fulfilled in its entirely.

Ezekiel 37 - The Valley of Dry Bones

Ezekiel 37:1-11 is the infamous chapter about the "Valley of Dry Bones" that describes the supernatural nature of the nation of Israel's existence. This prophecy declares that Israel as an exiled nation will be restored and raised from the dead. The dry bones coming together with sinew and flesh forming "an exceeding great army" spotlights God's restoration of Israel as a nation.

This chapter predicts the return of Israel back to its land after 2,000 years of exile. It pinpointed May 14, 1948 when the nation of Israel was to be established again as a nation among the world community of nations.

"Then say to them, 'Thus says the Lord God: "Surely I will take the children of Israel from among the nations, wherever they have gone, and will gather them from every side and bring them into their own land." Ezekiel 37:21

Because Ezekiel 38 & 39 follows Ezekiel 37, it appears that these chapters contain events that will take place approximately in the same period of time. We are living to see the fulfillment of these prophecies today.

Ezekiel 38,39 - The War of Armageddon

The Russian Alliance Identified

According to Ezekiel 38-39, Russia is identified as Magog, the father of today's Russian people, (38:1-3) and will lead a military alliance of nations.

The allies of Russia will constitute a "great company" (38:4-6) identified as Persia, Ethiopia, Libya, Gomer, Togarmah and many others. (Genesis 10:2)

Persia is the region called Iran. Libya is listed as an ally. Another in Russia's alliance is "Gomer," identified in Genesis 10:2-3 as one of the sons of Japheth and seems to point to China. China seems to be the nation, possibly along with others, that one day will release its two hundred million-men army across the Middle East. (Revelation 9:16)

Togarmah seems to indicate a region we find occupying Mongolia, Siberia and perhaps Manchuria and North Korea. (38:5,6) (Genesis 10:3)

Today's media headlines verify that these alliances exist as the Bible had previously predicted 2,500 years ago.

Nations Not Joining the Alliance

"Sheba and Dedan" (38:13) seem to point to the "Cushite nations" that are Western-friendly. (Genesis 10:7) "Ethiopia" is translated from "Cush" in Hebrew and seems to refer to Pakistan and India. Other Cushite nations are Afghanistan, Sri Lanka and Bangladesh.

Another "brown-skinned Cushite" nation close to the USA is the Philippines.

"Tarshish" (38:13) could refer to Japan ("Javan,", Genesis 10:40) and Indonesia ("Java"), a principal Islamic nation, could also be referenced. Sri Lanka, Bangladesh and India would not appear to be an adversary against the Western nations.

In Ezekiel 38:13, the "young lions" (38:13) could point to smaller Asian nations such as South Korea, Taiwan, Hong Kong and Singapore. These nations today are called the "Four Tiger Nations" of Asia and are friendly to Western powers.

Currently, these nations owe a great deal to the Western nations for their economic strength and would most likely not support the Russian Alliance.

The Nations Targeted by the Russian Alliance

Ezekiel 38-39 predicts that the Russian Alliance will attack the latter-day ten tribes of Israel and the modern nations of Ephraim and Manasseh. But who are the modern day 10 tribes and Ephraim and Manasseh?

Ezekiel 38:8,12 gives a clue. It will be a nation "gathered out of many people," a "melting pot" nation.

Joel 2:20-32 seems to point to a similar prophetic event and describes that nation as having a border on its "eastern" and a "western" sea coast.

But what modern nation is known as a "melting pot" nation with borders "from sea to shining sea"?

It seems that the United States fits most closely to that description and is the leading nation of the Western alliance and most hated by the Russian-led alliance.

Though many describe the land of Israel as the target of Russia's attack, the land in Ezekiel 38 & 39 is located between two seas and is a melting pot of nations. It seems more than likely to refer to the USA. That nation also "dwells in safety .. unwalled ...." (38:11, see next section *The Rationale...*)

But who are the two sons of Joseph?

Ephraim was the elder son of Joseph and due the birthright. But Jacob, Joseph's father, gave the birthright blessing to Joseph's younger son, Manasseh. (Genesis 48:13,14) Are there powerful brother nations today where the younger one has surpassed the older?

Yes. They are found in the European nations led by Great Britain, the older nation, and in the United States of America, their younger brother.

The USA is a great superpower nation and the younger brother of European nations. It is a melting pot nation and bordered by two oceans. The USA seems to fit the description of

Manasseh. Included in Great Britain's alliance of nations would be Canada, Australia, New Zealand, Scandinavia and other European nations.

This description of today's nations is in alignment with Ezekiel's prophecy of the last day alliances.

And the land of Israel is not ignored. Jeremiah 30 clearly includes Judah (the present land of Israel) as another target of the Russian Alliance. Zechariah 14 also highlights "Judah" in this war. It seems that an assault on the land of Israel will occur at the same time the USA and Europe are attacked in the "latter days". These prophetic grouping of nations are currently in alignment today.

The Rationale Behind the War

Ezekiel 38:10-12 gives us the motive behind this attack as to "take a spoil...cattle and goods." The motive is envy of the wealth of the West and its move towards disarming its military.

The Russian alliance will mistakenly think that the nations of the West have become "soft targets." They are described as "dwelling without walls" and "having neither bars nor gates" - a people who have foolishly "let down their defenses." (38:8,11) This imagery has accurately foretold the rapid disarmament by the Western nations since the "Cold War ended." This cannot refer to the land of Israel that is actively defending its borders and engaged in battle against Hamas and the Palestinians.

The Lord's Intervention & The Russian Defeat

The Russian assault will gain momentum because of the element of surprise. The Western nations will be at a disadvantage, fearful of their demise. They will cry out in desperation and the Lord will respond. (Joel 2:1,12,13,18)

A great earthquake will occur disabling the powers of their enemies. (38:19-21) This intervention parallels Joel 2:10,11 and other prophecies. Joel saw God himself shout at the head of a divine army that intervened to rescue Israel from a northern army. (Joel 2:20)

God will also plague the armies of Gog with "pestilence", which could refer to a chemical and bacteriological attack against Gog's armies. God will release "fire and brimstone" which is a description of a nuclear attack against the armies of Gog. (38:22)

Zechariah 14:12 describes what follows: "...their flesh shall consume away ... their eyes shall consume away in their holes ... their tongue shall consume away in their mouth." This seems to describe human beings caught in a nuclear explosion, people who literally "consume away" as they are still standing. The slaughter of Gog's alliance will not stop until only "a sixth part" of them are left. (Ezekiel 39:2, KJV)

The fowls of the air will be invited to "gather together for the supper of the great God." (Revelation19:17,18; Ezekiel 39:17-20)

The enemy will be conquered. God will declare the war over.

The End of the Age

God announces, "It is done!" in Ezekiel 39:8 after the events of Ezekiel 38-39. Armageddon is over. The anti-Christ's morally and financially corrupt systems have been decimated.

"It is done!" is also declared from God's throne in Revelation 16:11. The context shows these two chapters as parallel events.

Ezekiel 39:8 follows God's divine intervention in a great war on earth. These words are spoken in the wake of a massive global earthquake (Ezekiel 38:20).

The words "It is done" in Revelation 16:17 follow the same pattern. Jesus Christ's intervenes in the great war of "Armageddon" (Revelation 16:16) and releases an unprecedented earthquake (verse 18).

This age draws to a close and the curtain falls on this final stage of divine history planned before the beginning of time. The stage is set for the "new heaven and new earth" to begin. (Revelation 21:1)

[1] Summarized from Collins, Steven. *What Exekiel 38-39 Reveals*. 2005, South Dakota

APPENDIX XI
The 2ND Coming of Christ

Summary: In His 1st Coming, Jesus arrived quietly and anonymously. In His 2nd Coming, He will return as a Victorious King with a lightning flash, trumpet blast, seen by the whole world and accompanied by an army of billions of His followers.

The Secret Rapture: Is Jesus coming secretly to take His people at an unsuspecting time? Will unbelievers awaken one day to discover loved ones missing around the world? Will "one be taken and the other left" because of a secret rapture?

What does the scriptures teach on this subject?

Jesus' Teaching: (Matthew 24:1-31)

A Dramatic, Visible Event - Jesus Christ taught that His 2nd Coming would be a visible event capturing the world's attention. He described it as a flash of lightning illuminating the earth's sky.(v.30,31) It would include a celebration of public triumph and a military procession of heaven's armies. Angels would blare triumphant trumpet sounds. His return would be with great power and glory. His followers would join Him from the four corners of the earth.

These events hardly describe a silent occasion that would capture the world by surprise. Jesus describes events so dramatic the whole world will see them.

No hint of a secret rapture is given here, except for Him to teach, "Therefore if they say to you, 'Look, He is in the desert!' Do not go out... For as the lightning comes from the east and flashes to the west, so also will the coming of the Son of Man be." (v.26,27) Jesus taught a spectacular, jaw-dropping event.

Announced by Major Events - Jesus' description of events leading to His return are also so striking it would make the events difficult to miss.

Major catastrophes such as earthquakes, wars, epidemics and famines (v.3) that increase in frequency and intensity would announce His return. The message of His love and salvation would be preached to all nations. (v.14) His return would be accompanied by the unprecedented rise of false religions. (v.4,5) These are all indicators of His soon return.

None of these signs hint at events that can be ignored by any sensible person. These signs will be recognized by the whole world.

Paul's Teaching: (I Thessalonians 4:13-18)

Confirmed by the Apostle Paul - Paul's description parallels Jesus' words perfectly. He wrote of an event so dramatic no person would miss it.

Paul taught that Jesus Christ would return descending from heaven with a "shout" or, as translated in Greek means, "a loud military declaration of victory".(v.16) Jesus' coming would be accompanied by a "voice of the archangel" and with "the trumpet of God." And, as Jesus taught, the saints would be caught up and taken to meet Him in the air. (v.17)

Again, these events will be glaringly public events to be seen by every person and captured by news media around the world.

These descriptions of His return are based on classic passages taught throughout the history of the church.

What About The "Secret Rapture?"

If the Bible is so clear about obvious signs of His return, how do we explain passages that teach a "secret rapture?"

"The Thief in the Night" - I Thessalonians 5:2 says, "For you yourselves know perfectly that the day of the Lord so comes as a thief in the night." This verse has been the source used to document the secret rapture. It is taught that Jesus will come and snatch His people at an unsuspecting time in a secret rapture.

What is quoted is accurate but, when read in its context, it conveys a different message.

To whom will He come as a "thief in the night?" Normally, we interpret it to mean the believers. But the scripture says a different thing.

"But you, brethren, are not in darkness, so that this Day should overtake you as a thief." (v.4) "You are all sons of light and sons of the day." (v.5) God' s people will not be surprised but those in darkness will be.

Jesus is coming to the unbelieving world, not the church, as a thief.

"Come Up Here!" - Revelation 4:1 is used as a key verse calling the church in a secret rapture. But what is the context in which this verse is used?

This verse isn't a call to the church but a call to John. John is called into heaven to catch a glimpse of earth's prophetic future. Nothing is said of the church being whisked away. John is called to the unveiling of prophecy, not a secret rapture.

The Book of Revelation contains the only passage that parallels the 2nd Coming teachings of Jesus and Paul. That passage is found in Revelation 19:11-16. All Bible teachers unanimously accept that passage as a clear teaching of the return of Jesus Christ to the world. This passage clearly describes this event as a public, spectacular and climactic event the world will witness. It will not be a secret event.

"One Taken, One Left" - Matthew 24:36-44 describes a scenario associated with Jesus' teaching on His second coming. He teaches that two will be in the field and two grinding at the mill, but one will be taken and the other left.

The popular interpretation of this passage is that the one taken is the believer and the one left is the unbeliever. But we must ask ourselves: "Does the context validate that interpretation?"

To begin with, we must ask the question: "Where are they being taken to?" That is the exact question that the disciple asked Jesus as He was teaching them. (Luke 17:37a) Jesus' answer to "Where" will answer the question "Who."

1) *They were being swept away in the flood of judgment.* Matthew 24:37-39 "But as the days of Noah were, so also will the coming of the Son of Man be.. And did not know until the Flood came and *took them all away,* so also will the coming of the Son of Man be." Who was "taken away" in the flood of Noah? It was those who "...did not know until the Flood came..." The next verse says, "Then two men will be in the field: one will be taken and the other left." (v.40)It was the unbelievers, not the believers, who were taken away in the flood.

2) *"Where the carcasses are ... the vultures gather together."* (Luke 17:37b) This is the answer Jesus gives His disciples when they asked for clarification, "Where are they being taken to?" He answered them, "They will be taken to where the vultures gather."

So, now, we need to ask the question: "Where do the vultures gather around the bodies of the dead?"

The answer is found in Revelation 19:17-21. This refers to the coming of Jesus Christ and the War of Armageddon. An invitation is given to the birds of prey to feast on bodies of the dead gathered to war against Jesus and His army in the final battle of all of history. The "Where" is a place of war and judgment.

"Come and gather together for the supper of the great God that you may eat of the flesh of kings, the flesh of horses ... and the flesh of all people, free, and slave, both small and great."

People are "being taken away" to become the dinner meal for the birds of prey invited to the feast.

When Will Jesus Return?

After Two Events Occur - In 2 Thessalonians 2:1-4, Paul teaches clearly that Jesus' return will not happen unless two events occur:

1*)" The Falling Away"* (v.2a) of believers of Christ. This can only happen after they have been converted to Christ. So this event point to a worldwide revival but multitudes will recant from their faith in times of persecution. And,

2) *"The Man of Sin is Revealed."* (v.2b) This person is also called the son of perdition. This is a definite reference to the Anti-Christ who will arise in the last days described and defined in Revelation 13.

At The Last Trump - I Corinthians 15:51,52 clearly tells us the coming of the Lord will be "at the last trump." Paul makes that point very clear. So, we need to ask ourselves when that last trumpet will sound?

Revelation explains 7th or last Trumpet sounding.

In Revelation 8 & 9, John describes Seven Trumpet Judgments emerging out of the Seven Seal Judgments. Then, Revelation 10:7 describes 7th or last Trumpet.

"But in the days of the sounding of the 7th angel, when he is about to sound, the mystery of God would be finished."

John writes that the 7th or last Trumpet will "begin to sound" and will pave the way for the return of Jesus Christ in Revelation 19. Evidently, this isn't an event that occurs and is over. This trumpet is one that continuously blasts over a period of time.

It appears that the events of Revelation 11-18 cover that period of time leading up to the conclusion of the 7th Trumpet's blast in the return of Jesus Christ to the earth.

APPENDIX XII
THE ABRAHAMIC COVENANT
- A Study of Galatians 3 -

***Summary*:** God established the Abrahamic Covenant of Grace, then inserted the Mosaic Covenant of Law for a 1,500 years period and finally fulfilled and reinstated the Abrahamic Covenant of Grace through Jesus Christ.

Introduction

A misconception exists in Christian circles regarding the Covenant of Grace.

Many believe that God was a God of Law in the Old Testament and that, in the New Testament for the first time Jesus Christ introduced a God of Grace. Nothing could be further from the truth.

God never changes. The Bible claims Him to be "… the same yesterday, today and forever." (Hebrews 13:8) He is first and foremost a God of Grace.

That is how He revealed Himself to Abraham.

The apostles well understood that thought.

Paul called Abraham "the father of the faith" (Romans 4:11,12) because he was a forerunner of New Testament believers. The apostle Paul called believers "children of Abraham" (Galatians 3:7,29) because they and Abraham had a common revelation of God.

Abraham and New Testament believers were linked together because of the common revelation of the God of grace.

The Abrahamic Covenant of Grace

The apostle Paul makes it abundantly clear that the good news of God's grace was introduced to Abraham in the Old Testament and explained how that message was promised to have a global impact in the future.

"And the scripture, foreseeing that God would justify the heathen through faith, preached before the gospel to Abraham, [saying], In you shall all nations be blessed." (Galatians 3:8)

Not only did Paul verify Abraham's revelation of the gospel, even Jesus in His teachings validated that event when He said, "Your father Abraham rejoiced to see my day, and saw it, and was glad." (John 8:56) Though he lived in the Old Testament era, Abraham saw the day of the incarnation of Jesus Christ and the Good News His life would bring on earth.

Paul also explains that Abraham not only understood a general message of God's love, but that he also understood that righteousness was a gift through faith, not achieved by works through the law.

"He ... that ministers ... the Spirit ... [does he do it] by the works of the law, or by the hearing of faith? Even as Abraham believed God, and it was accounted to him for righteousness." Galatians 3:5,6

Paul further clarifies this in the Book of Romans as he explains how God introduced circumcision to Abraham and demanded it under the Mosaic Law. Paul contends that Abraham received grace ("justified by faith") before he was instructed about and applied the "rite of circumcision." Abraham experienced acceptance by God through grace before obeying God in the act of circumcision.

"And he received ... the righteousness of the faith which he had yet being uncircumcised: that he might be the father of all them that believe ... that righteousness might be imputed unto them also..." Romans 4:11; Genesis 15:6; 17:10,11)

Paul makes it clear that Abraham was justified by faith as a model for New Testament believers.

Paul also taught that the promise of a "seed" given to Abraham pointed, not to Isaac, but to the coming Messiah, Jesus Christ, who would be the ultimate fulfillment of God's promised seed.

"Now to Abraham and his seed were the promises made. He saith not, And to seeds, as of many; but as of one, And to thy seed, which is Christ." Galatians 3:16

So, Paul's writing clearly documents that Abraham experienced the God of Grace. But that leaves us a question: "Where did the Mosaic Law fit in the Old Testament?" "Why was the Covenant of Law given?"

The Covenant of Law

Paul addresses the role of the Mosaic Law in Galatians 3. He teaches that the Mosaic Law did not supersede or cancel the Abrahamic Covenant of Grace.

"And this I say, [that] the covenant [of Grace to Abraham], that was confirmed before of God in Christ, the law, which was four hundred and thirty years after, cannot disannul, that it should make the promise[of righteousness by faith] of none effect." Galatians 3:17

Then, he adds, that the Mosaic Law was inserted in the plan of God because of Israel's sin. It was not a predesigned intention by God in His plan for history.

"Wherefore then [serves] the law? It was *added* because of transgressions, till the seed should come to whom the promise was made; [and it was] ordained by angels in the hand of a mediator." Galatians 3:19

So, the Law was added as a temporary measure until God's full purpose could be accomplished to fulfill and reinstate the Abrahamic Covenant through Jesus Christ. And for what purpose was the Law added?

The purpose of the Law was clear. It was to reveal man's inadequacy in living up to God's standard. Man's inadequacy would reveal his need to depend on God's grace and love instead of his own works.

"Wherefore the law was our schoolmaster to bring us to Christ ...[to] be justified by faith." Galatians 3:24

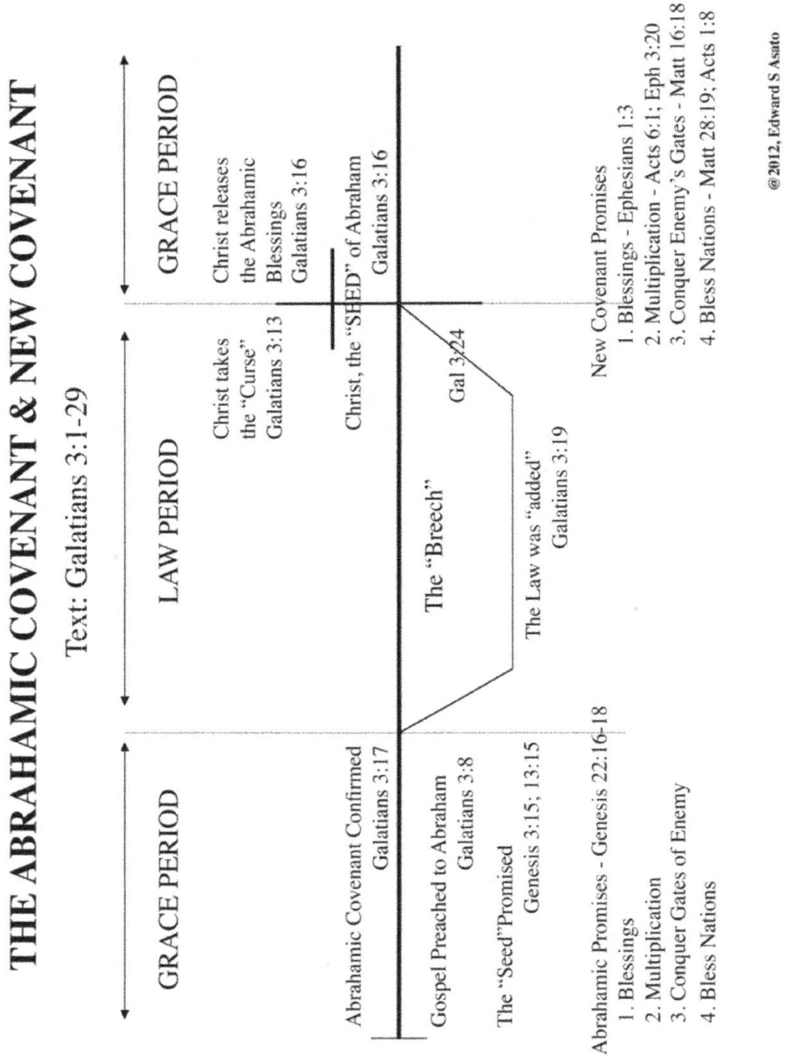

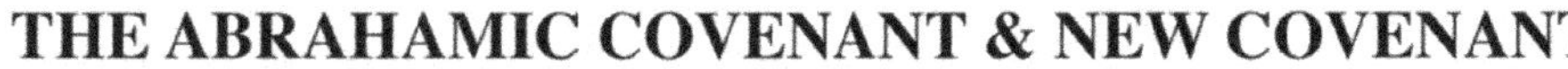

THE ABRAHAMIC COVENANT & NEW COVENANT
Text: Galatians 3:1-29
GRACE PERIOD
LAW PERIOD
GRACE PERIOD
Abrahamic Covenant Confirmed
Galatians 3:17
Gospel Preached to Abraham
Galatians 3:8
The "Seed"Promised
Genesis 3:15; 13:15
Abrahamic Promises - Genesis 22:16-18
1. Blessings
2. Multiplication
3. Conquer Gates of Enemy
4. Bless Nations
The "Breech"
The Law was "added"
Galatians 3:19
Gal 3:24
Christ takes
the "Curse"
Galatians 3:13
Christ, the "SEED" of Abraham
Galatians 3:16
Christ releases
the Abrahamic
Blessings
Galatians 3:16
New Covenant Promises
1. Blessings - Ephesians 1:3
2. Multiplication - Acts 6:1; Eph 3:20
3. Conquer Enemy's Gates - Matt 16:18
4. Bless Nations - Matt 28:19; Acts 1:8
@2012, Edward S Asato

The Abrahamic Covenant Fulfilled & Reinstated

The New Testament Covenant was based on Jesus' death on the cross. His death would atone for man's sins so God's abundant grace and His gift of righteousness could be accessed. (Romans 5:17) Jesus took upon Himself the curse of the law and freed us from the consequences of that law.

"Christ has redeemed us from the curse of the law, being made a curse for us: for it is written , Cursed is every one that hangs on a tree:" Galatians 3:13

The Law which was inserted in God's plan could now be legally removed. And what happens next is something few believers understand of God's purposes.

With the Law dealt with, God could now reinstate what He began in His relationship with Abraham.

Paul makes clear that because of the cross, New Testament believer could access all of the promises God made with Abraham.

"That the blessing of Abraham might come on the Gentiles through Jesus Christ; that we might receive the promise of the Spirit through faith." Galatians 3:14

Paul explains that the Abrahamic Covenant and the New Covenant are one of the same. Both reveal a God of love and grace, not a God of works and law.

Paul concludes Galatians 3 with the thought "... if you belong to Christ, then are you Abraham's seed and heirs according to the promise." Galatians 3:29

At the same time that Jesus Christ became the fulfillment of the promised "seed" to Abraham, He also reinstated the Abrahamic Covenant of Grace to New Testament believers.

The diagram on page 110 explains this teaching in a more simplified picture.

BIBLIOGRAPHY

Alcorn, Randy. *Heaven.* Illinois: Tyndale House, 2007
Cahn, Jonathan. *The Harbinger*. Florida: Frontline Pub, 2012
Chumney, Edward. *The Seven Festivals of the Messiah*, Pennsylvania: Treasure House, 1994
Collins, Steven. *Israel's Tribes Today.* Michigan: Bible Blessings, 2005
Collins, Steven. *What Exekiel 38-39 Reveals.* 2005, South Dakota
Conner, Kevin J. *The Seventy Weeks Prophecy*. Victoria, Australia: Acacia Press Pty, Ltd, 1981
Conner, Kevin J. *Interpreting the Book of Revelation*. Portland: Bible Temple Publishing, 1995
Conner, Kevin J. *The Book of Revelation*. Victoria, Australia: K.J.C. Publications, 2001
Conner, Kevin J. *Relevance Of Old Testament To New Testament Church*. Portland, OR: City Bible Publishing, 1986
Graff, Ron & Dolphin, Lambert. *Connecting the Dots*. Maitland, Florida: Xulon Press, 2010
Hagee, John. *Earth's Final Moments*. Florida: Charisma House, 2011
Jeremiah, David. *What in the World is Going On?.* Tennessee: Thomas Nelson, 2008
Jeremiah, David. *The Coming Economic Armageddon.* New York: Hachette Book Group, 2010
Ladd, George. *The Blessed Hope*. Michigan: Wm. B. Eerdmans Publishing Co, 1956
Lindsey, Hal. *The Late Great Planet Earth*. Michigan, Zondervan, 1970
Lindsey, Hal. Faith *for Earth's Final Hour*. Murrieta, California: Oracle House Publishing, 2003
MacPherson, Dave. *The Incredible Cover-Up.* Plainfield, New Jersey: Logos International, 1975
McTernan, John P. *As America Has Done To Israel.* Pennsylvania: Whitaker House, 2008

Panin, Ivan. *Bible Numerics*. Surprise, Arizona: Berean Publishers, 1914

Panin, Ivan. *The Writings of Ivan Panin*". Forgotten Books, 2012

Panin, Ivan. *The Inspiration of Scriptures Scientifically Demonstrated.* New York Sun, 1899 http://www.telusplanet.net/public/tsgibson/panin.pdf

Pentecost, Dwight J. *Things to Come*. Michigan: Zondervan, 1958

Rosenberg, Joel. *Implosion*. Illinois: Tyndale House Publishers Inc, 2012

Scott, Bruce. *The Feasts of Israel.* New Jersey: Friends of Israel,1997

Tenny, Merrill, C. *Interpreting Revelation.* Michigan: Wm. B. Eerdmans Publishing Co, 1988

Wilkerson, David. *The Vision and Beyond.* Texas: World Challenge Publications, 2003

Wohlberg, Steve & Roberts, Charles H. *End Time Delusions*. Pennsylvania: Treasure House, 2005

www.ingramcontent.com/pod-product-compliance
Lightning Source LLC
Chambersburg PA
CBHW051814040426
42446CB00007B/661

* 9 7 8 0 6 1 5 7 6 9 9 0 5 *